JULIO IGLESIAS

JULIO IGLESIAS

Elizabeth Martino

CHELSEA HOUSE PUBLISHERS
NEW YORK ■ PHILADELPHIA

CHELSEA HOUSE PUBLISHERS

Editorial Director: Richard Rennert
Executive Managing Editor: Karyn Gullen Browne
Copy Chief: Robin James
Picture Editor: Adrian G. Allen
Art Director: Robert Mitchell
Manufacturing Director: Gerald Levine

HISPANICS OF ACHIEVEMENT
Senior Editor: Philip Koslow

Staff for *JULIO IGLESIAS*
Copy Editor: Joy Sanchez
Assistant Editor: Mary B. Sisson
Designer: M. Cambraia Magalhães
Picture Researcher: Ellen Barrett Dudley
Cover Illustrator: Andrea Lannin

3 5 7 9 8 6 4 2

Library of Congress Cataloging-in-Publication Data
Martino, Elizabeth.
Julio Iglesias / Elizabeth Martino.
p. cm.—(Hispanics of achievement)
0-7910-2017-7
0-7910-2018-5 (pbk.)
1. Iglesias, Julio, 1943——Juvenile literature. 2. Singers—Spain—Biography—Juvenile literature. [1. Iglesias, Julio, 1943– . 2. Singers.] I. Series.
ML3930.I4M37 1994
782.42164'092—dc20
94-1932
[B]
CIP
AC MN

CONTENTS

HISPANICS OF ACHIEVEMENT

JOAN BAEZ
Mexican-American folksinger

RUBÉN BLADES
Panamanian lawyer and entertainer

JORGE LUIS BORGES
Argentine writer

PABLO CASALS
Spanish cellist and conductor

MIGUEL DE CERVANTES
Spanish writer

CESAR CHAVEZ
Mexican-American labor leader

JULIO CÉSAR CHÁVEZ
Mexican boxing champion

EL CID
Spanish military leader

HENRY CISNEROS
Mexican-American political leader

ROBERTO CLEMENTE
Puerto Rican baseball player

SALVADOR DALÍ
Spanish painter

PLÁCIDO DOMINGO
Spanish singer

GLORIA ESTEFAN
Cuban-American singer

GABRIEL GARCÍA MÁRQUEZ
Colombian writer

FRANCISCO JOSÉ DE GOYA
Spanish painter

JULIO IGLESIAS
Spanish singer

RAUL JULIA
Puerto Rican actor

FRIDA KAHLO
Mexican painter

JOSÉ MARTÍ
Cuban revolutionary and poet

RITA MORENO
Puerto Rican singer and actress

PABLO NERUDA
Chilean poet and diplomat

OCTAVIO PAZ
Mexican poet and critic

PABLO PICASSO
Spanish artist

ANTHONY QUINN
Mexican-American actor

DIEGO RIVERA
Mexican painter

LINDA RONSTADT
Mexican-American singer

ANTONIO LÓPEZ DE SANTA ANNA
Mexican general and politician

GEORGE SANTAYANA
Spanish philosopher and poet

JUNÍPERO SERRA
Spanish missionary and explorer

LEE TREVINO
Mexican-American golfer

PANCHO VILLA
Mexican revolutionary

CHELSEA HOUSE PUBLISHERS

HISPANICS OF ACHIEVEMENT

Rodolfo Cardona

The Spanish language and many other elements of Spanish culture are present in the United States today and have been since the country's earliest beginnings. Some of these elements have come directly from the Iberian Peninsula; others have come indirectly, by way of Mexico, the Caribbean basin, and the countries of Central and South America.

Spanish culture has influenced America in many subtle ways, and consequently many Americans remain relatively unaware of the extent of its impact. The vast majority of them recognize the influence of Spanish culture in America, but they often do not realize the great importance and long history of that influence. This is partly because Americans have tended to judge the Hispanic influence in the United States in statistical terms rather than to look closely at the ways in which individual Hispanics have profoundly affected American culture. For this reason, it is fitting that Americans obtain more than a passing acquaintance with the origins of these Spanish cultural elements and gain an understanding of how they have been woven into the fabric of American society.

It is well documented that Spanish seafarers were the first to explore and colonize many of the early territories of what is today called the United States of America. For this reason, students of geography discover Hispanic names all over the map of the United States. For instance, the Strait of Juan de Fuca was named after the Spanish explorer who first navigated the waters of the Pacific Northwest; the names of states such as Arizona (arid zone), Montana (mountain), Florida (thus named because it was reached on Easter Sunday, which in Spanish is called the feast of Pascua Florida), and California (named after a fictitious land in one of the first and probably the most popular among the Spanish novels of chivalry, *Amadis of Gaul*) are all derived from Spanish; and there are numerous mountains, rivers, canyons, towns, and cities with Spanish names throughout the United States.

Not only explorers but many other illustrious figures in Spanish history have helped define American culture. For example, the 13th-century king of Spain, Alfonso X, also known as the Learned, may be unknown to the majority of Americans, but his work on the codification of Spanish law has greatly influenced the evolution of American law, particularly in the jurisdictions of the Southwest. For this contribution a statue of him stands in the rotunda of the Capitol in Washington, D.C. Likewise, the name Diego Rivera may be unfamiliar to most Americans, but this Mexican painter influenced many American artists whose paintings, commissioned during the Great Depression and the New Deal era of the 1930s, adorn the walls of government buildings throughout the United States. In recent years the contributions of Puerto Ricans, Mexicans, Mexican Americans (Chicanos), and Cubans in American cities such as Boston, Chicago, Los Angeles, Miami, Minneapolis, New York, and San Antonio have been enormous.

The importance of the Spanish language in this vast cultural complex cannot be overstated. Spanish, after all, is second only to English as the most widely spoken of Western languages within the United States as well as in the entire world. The popularity of the Spanish language in America has a long history.

In addition to Spanish exploration of the New World, the great Spanish literary tradition served as a vehicle for bringing the language and culture to America. Interest in Spanish literature in America began when English immigrants brought with them translations of Spanish masterpieces of the Golden Age. As early as 1683, private libraries in Philadelphia and Boston contained copies of the first picaresque novel, *Lazarillo de Tormes*, translations of Francisco de Quevedo's *Los Sueños*, and copies of the immortal epic of reality and illusion *Don Quixote*, by the great Spanish writer Miguel de Cervantes. It would not be surprising if Cotton Mather, the arch-Puritan, read *Don Quixote* in its original Spanish, if only to enrich his vocabulary in preparation for his writing *La fe del cristiano en 24 artículos de la Institución de Cristo, enviada a los españoles para que abran sus ojos* (The Christian's Faith in 24 Articles of the Institution of Christ, Sent to the Spaniards to Open Their Eyes), published in Boston in 1699.

Over the years, Spanish authors and their works have had a vast influence on American literature—from Washington Irving, John Steinbeck, and Ernest Hemingway in the novel to Henry Wadsworth Longfellow and Archibald MacLeish in poetry. Such important American writers as James Fenimore Cooper, Edgar Allan Poe, Walt Whitman, Mark Twain, and Herman Melville all owe a sizable debt to the Spanish literary tradition. Some writers, such as Willa Cather and Maxwell Anderson, who explored Spanish themes they came into contact with in the American Southwest and Mexico, were influenced less directly but no less profoundly.

Important contributions to a knowledge of Spanish culture in the United States were also made by many lesser known individuals—teachers, publishers, historians, entrepreneurs, and others—with a love for Spanish culture. One of the most significant of these contributions was made by Abiel Smith, a Harvard College graduate of the class of 1764, when he bequeathed stock worth $20,000 to Harvard for the support of a professor of French and Spanish. By 1819 this endowment had produced enough income to appoint a professor, and the philologist and humanist George Ticknor became the first holder of the Abiel

Smith Chair, which was the very first endowed Chair at Harvard University. Other illustrious holders of the Smith Chair would include the poets Henry Wadsworth Longfellow and James Russell Lowell.

A highly respected teacher and scholar, Ticknor was also a collector of Spanish books, and as such he made a very special contribution to America's knowledge of Spanish culture. He was instrumental in amassing for Harvard libraries one of the first and most impressive collections of Spanish books in the United States. He also had a valuable personal collection of Spanish books and manuscripts, which he bequeathed to the Boston Public Library.

With the creation of the Abiel Smith Chair, Spanish language and literature courses became part of the curriculum at Harvard, which also went on to become the first American university to offer graduate studies in Romance languages. Other colleges and universities throughout the United States gradually followed Harvard's example, and today Spanish language and culture may be studied at most American institutions of higher learning.

No discussion of the Spanish influence in the United States, however brief, would be complete without a mention of the Spanish influence on art. Important American artists such as John Singer Sargent, James A. M. Whistler, Thomas Eakins, and Mary Cassatt all explored Spanish subjects and experimented with Spanish techniques. Virtually every serious American artist living today has studied the work of the Spanish masters as well as the great 20th-century Spanish painters Salvador Dalí, Joan Miró, and Pablo Picasso.

The most pervasive Spanish influence in America, however, has probably been in music. Compositions such as Leonard Bernstein's *West Side Story*, the Latinization of William Shakespeare's *Romeo and Juliet* set in New York's Puerto Rican quarter, and Aaron Copland's *Salon Mexico* are two obvious examples. In general, one can hear the influence of Latin rhythms—from tango to mambo, from guaracha to salsa—in virtually every form of American music.

This series of biographies, which Chelsea House has published under the general title HISPANICS OF ACHIEVEMENT, constitutes further recognition of—and a renewed effort to bring forth to the consciousness of America's young people—the contributions that Hispanic people have made not only in the United States but throughout the civilized world. The men and women who are featured in this series have attained a high level of accomplishment in their respective fields of endeavor and have made a permanent mark on American society.

The title of this series must be understood in its broadest possible sense: The term *Hispanics* is intended to include Spaniards, Spanish Americans, and individuals from many countries whose language and culture have either direct or indirect Spanish origins. The names of many of the people included in this series will be immediately familiar; others will be less recognizable. All, however, have attained recognition within their own countries, and often their fame has transcended their borders.

The series HISPANICS OF ACHIEVEMENT thus addresses the attainments and struggles of Hispanic people in the United States and seeks to tell the stories of individuals whose personal and professional lives in some way reflect the larger Hispanic experience. These stories are exemplary of what human beings can accomplish, often against daunting odds and by extraordinary personal sacrifice, where there is conviction and determination. Fray Junípero Serra, the 18th-century Spanish Franciscan missionary, is one such individual. Although in very poor health, he devoted the last 15 years of his life to the foundation of missions throughout California—then a mostly unsettled expanse of land—in an effort to bring a better life to Native Americans through the cultivation of crafts and animal husbandry. An example from recent times, the Mexican-American labor leader Cesar Chavez battled bitter opposition and made untold personal sacrifices in his effort to help poor agricultural workers who have been exploited for decades on farms throughout the Southwest.

The talent with which each one of these men and women may have been endowed required dedication and hard work to develop and become fully realized. Many of them have enjoyed rewards for their efforts during their own lifetime, whereas others have died poor and unrecognized. For some it took a long time to achieve their goals, for others success came at an early age, and for still others the struggle continues. All of them, however, stand out as people whose lives have made a difference, whose achievements we need to recognize today and should continue to honor in the future.

JULIO IGLESIAS

"I FELT
LIKE I HAD DIED"

On a warm night in 1963, four young men were jammed into in a small red sports car that was zipping along a winding two-lane road in the open country outside Madrid, Spain. They had just left a little village called Majadahonda, where they had attended a fiesta, or local festival. In the summer and early fall, many villages and towns in Spain hold their annual fiestas: the main street is decorated with lights and banners, and residents and visitors gather for several days of eating, drinking, amusements, and religious celebrations. For young people especially, the fiestas present an opportunity to have some fun and meet members of the opposite sex.

The four young men in the sports car—Pedro Luis Iglesias, Tito Arroyo, Enrique Clemente, and Julio Iglesias—were returning to their homes in Madrid, Spain's capital, in a very cheerful mood. They were not drunk, but they had absorbed the high spirits of the festival, and they shared the pleasure of being free to stay out as late as they wished. The driver of the car, Julio Iglesias (not related to Pedro Luis), was especially jubilant, and he had every reason to be. At the age of 20, he had nearly everything he could have wanted. His father was a successful doctor, and the Iglesias family enjoyed a comfortable life in Madrid. The little

Julio Iglesias in concert at New York's Radio City Music Hall in 1984. Called the world's most popular singer, Iglesias has recorded albums in six languages and has sold more than 160 million records.

15

sports car was Julio's own, a gift from his father. Better still, Julio had the chance to fulfill every young Spaniard's dream—to be a soccer star.

Tall and solidly built, Julio was also gifted with strength, speed, and agility. At the age of 12, he had been able to hold his own on the soccer field with boys of 16 and 17. At the age of 19, he was the goalkeeper for the junior team of Real Madrid, Spain's number one soccer club. He could realistically hope that before long he might be Real Madrid's starting goalkeeper, and perhaps even have a chance to play for Spain in the World Cup.

Like many young men in the prime of life, Julio never considered the idea that anything bad could happen to him. For that reason, he gunned his new car up to 80 miles an hour on the narrow, winding road, feeling the excitement of speed and danger. The road was paved with fine gravel. As Iglesias later recalled in his autobiography, *Entre el cielo y el infierno* (Between Heaven and Hell), he enjoyed looking in the rearview mirror and seeing a shower of tiny stones trailing the speeding car like a smoke cloud. "I was driving like a stupid, crazy guy," he later admitted.

As the car approached an especially sharp curve, Tito Arroyo, who was sitting next to Julio, became alarmed. "Be careful, Julio!" he said. "Slow down a little, take your foot off the gas, this is a dangerous curve."

In his supreme self-confidence, Julio shrugged off his friend's warning, boasting that he could handle the curve even better than Juan Manuel Fangio, the current world-champion racing driver. He put his foot down on the accelerator. But in the middle of the curve, he suddenly realized what he was dealing with. The bend in the highway was no mere turn—it was shaped like a horseshoe. As the little car struggled to hold the road, the tremendous strain on the wheels

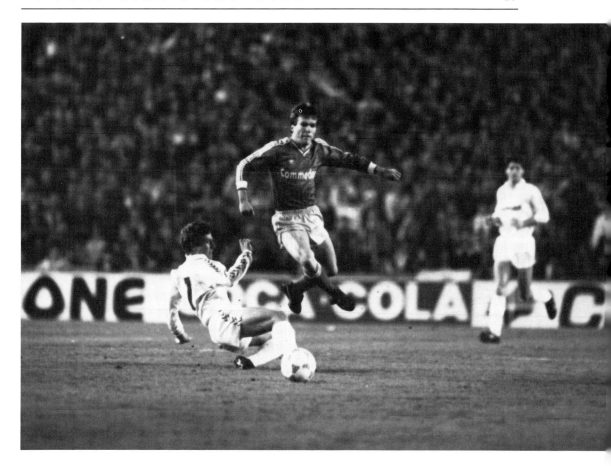

Real Madrid's Emilio Butragueño (left) strips the ball from an opponent during the 1988 European Champions' Cup match. Iglesias, a talented athlete in his youth, had a promising future with Madrid's illustrious soccer team before a spinal injury ended his career.

wrenched the steering wheel right out of Julio's grasp. The car spun out, crashed through a guardrail, and plunged into a nearby field, where it turned over several times before coming to a violent stop.

All three passengers were thrown clear of the car, escaping through the open windows. Julio, who had been "clinging to the steering wheel like a wild animal," crawled out of the demolished car, which was almost split in half, though the lights were still on and the radio continued to play, accompanying the crickets that sang in the silent fields. Miraculously, no one appeared to be seriously hurt. One of the young men had a cut on his face, another had bruised his leg, but they were all able to walk away from the accident.

Julio himself appeared to have emerged without a scratch.

Leaving the remains of the car, the four friends walked to a nearby town and found a bar with a telephone. Julio phoned his father's clinic, grateful that his father would not be there at such an hour of the morning, and the staff arranged for a car to pick the young men up. They were examined at the clinic, treated, and released. Julio arrived home at 4:00 A.M., bringing his startled parents news of the accident.

Dr. Iglesias gave his son a stern lecture but soon forgot the incident, and Julio went back to playing soccer without a second thought. Two or three weeks later, however, he began to feel that something was wrong. His reflexes, all-important for a goalkeeper, were not quite as sharp as they had been. Julio's coach thought that his young star was getting overconfident and a bit lazy, but Julio knew that this was not the case. "Something happened to me that night," he told his father.

Dr. Iglesias was concerned enough to send his son for tests and X rays. Still, the doctors failed to pinpoint any physical ailment. They suggested that Julio's increasing complaints about muscle fatigue and back pain might be psychological. They gave him pills to calm his nerves. But the pain got worse, so much so that Julio actually passed out one day walking in the street. In December, when snow fell in Madrid, he found himself slipping repeatedly. By Christmas, he had lost most of the sensation in his legs. "I was thinking I was going crazy," he recalled. "And by January, I couldn't walk, even in the house."

On January 6, 1964, Julio Iglesias entered the hospital. There the doctors finally discovered what was wrong with him. The impact of the automobile crash had caused internal bleeding near the base of his spine, and the bleeding compressed Julio's spinal cord. Surgeons operated on Julio for eight hours in an effort to relieve the pressure, but the damage was already done. "When I woke up," Julio recalled, "the first thing I remember is seeing my mother and father crying. I reached down and touched my leg, and there was no movement. It was completely paralyzed. The first re-action I had was, 'Why me?' . . . Being such an athlete, strong like a bull, and suddenly I have no legs. And I can move my hands only a little. I was 20 years old and thinking this was for life. I felt like I had died."

Fortunately, Julio's spirits quickly rebounded. A few days after the operation, he asked his father for some medical books so that he could read about his condition. As he studied the books, he understood that he had no reason to give up hope. His spine had been severely damaged; but as long as the spine had not been severed, there was the chance of at least a partial recovery. He made up his mind to do everything possible to get back on his feet.

Dr. Iglesias was equally determined to see his son walking. For the first year following the operation, he was with Julio all the time, completely neglecting his medical practice. Because of his immobility, Julio's muscles dwindled until his weight dropped from 185 pounds to less than 100. But after two months, Julio was finally able to move one of the toes on his left foot. After that breakthrough, he began doing exer-cises that were designed to restore the feeling and movement in his legs. He refused to try a wheelchair, crutches, or a walker. "At night, when my mother and father went to sleep," he remembered, "I jumped from the bed to the floor and walked like a dog all over the house. I didn't want anyone to see me. I only slept four or five hours a day. Everything else was exercise."

After a year of hard work, Julio was able to walk with the aid of two canes, and two years after that, at the age of 23, he was almost fully recovered. His goalkeeping days were over for good, but he now had a new interest in life—music.

This surprising development was a direct result of his illness. While growing up, Julio had never taken any serious interest in music and never felt that he had any real talent. In fact, when he tried out for the choir at his school at the age of 15, the choirmaster had turned him down. When he was confined to bed, however, he found that his physical limitations caused

Nineteen-year-old Julio Iglesias poses with his father, Dr. Julio Iglesias Puga, outside the house of the legendary bullfighter Manolete. When Julio was stricken with paralysis following a spinal operation, Dr. Iglesias gave up his medical practice for a year and devoted himself to his son's recovery.

his other senses to become sharper, so that colors and sounds appeared more vivid. Then one of his father's assistants gave Julio a guitar and a music book so that he could strengthen his hands and fingers, which had still not recovered their dexterity. After he learned the basic notes and chords, Julio began to accompany the singers he saw on the television in his hospital room. Before long, he was making up his own songs and singing them to his mother and father.

Though the music gave him pleasure and aided his recovery, Julio was not yet thinking of a musical career. He was convinced that singers were born with an obvious talent, and he had not been gifted in this way. Nevertheless, he was regaining his strength little by little, and eventually he would have to find an outlet for his youthful energies. "I did know," he recalled, "that I needed lights. Applause. I knew success already from sports. I couldn't do sports again, yet I knew I couldn't survive without lights."

From that need developed a singing career that took Julio Iglesias all over the world, created more than 60 record albums, and resulted in sales of more than 160 million recordings, more than any other artist of his day. It has been estimated that every 30 seconds one of Iglesias's songs is played on the radio somewhere in the world. This phenomenal success represents a remarkable turnaround for a man who had felt at the age of 20 that his life might be over. In fact, it was just beginning.

"SINGING IS NOT YOUR THING"

When Julio José Iglesias de la Cueva was born in a Madrid hospital on September 23, 1943, his mother, Rosario de la Cueva y Iglesias, claimed that she heard him cry out even before he was delivered. This memory of his mother's made a deep impression on the young Julio. In Spain, some people believed that infants who were heard to cry out while still in the womb were destined to achieve great things but also to be solitary figures, never satisfied with their lives or their accomplishments.

Romantic ideas such as this were not typical of the well-to-do professional class into which Julio was born. They had their roots in the heritage of his father, Dr. Julio Iglesias Puga. Though well established in Madrid as a gynecologist and obstetrician who had himself delivered thousands of babies, Dr. Iglesias had been born and raised in the province of Galicia, a land of legend and romance.

The province of Galicia occupies the northwestern corner of Spain, bordering the Atlantic Ocean on the west and the Bay of Biscay in the north. In many ways, Galicia is the most intriguing of all Spain's regions; it also differs most radically from the customary image of Spain as a hot, dry, sun-baked land.

Galicia, by contrast, is mountainous, wooded, and green, generally pleasant in the summer but damp and misty in the winter. The inhabitants of the region are mostly Celtic in ancestry: they are descended from the same ancient people that settled in Ireland, Scotland, Wales, and the province of Brittany in France. Like all Celts, Galicians are great seafarers and adventurers. Today, the rugged Galician coast is still dotted with fishing villages.

During the summers of Julio's early years, the Iglesias family vacationed in the coastal town of Cangas, where he absorbed impressions that remained with him for the rest of his life. Though he also identified with the heritage of his mother, who traced her roots to the southern Spanish province of Andalusia and the island of Puerto Rico in the Caribbean Sea, Julio strongly felt that he was above all a Galician. "Galicia is the place where I ought to have been born," he later wrote. He felt himself Galician to the core: "I am loyal. A tireless worker. A little suspicious. A very private person, but a lover of foreign lands. I have been, and still am, a fortunate pilgrim . . . one who left his home one day with a suitcase looking far and wide for the gold that he could not find in his own land."

Throughout their history, Galicians have been proud and independent. For example, when the Moors from North Africa overran Spain during the 8th century, Galicia—protected by its dense forests and mountainous terrain—was one of the few regions the invaders failed to conquer. Much of Spain remained under Moorish control until the 15th century, absorbing the culture, customs, and architecture of the East, but Galicia retained its original character. Even today, Galicians continue to speak their own language (which closely resembles Portuguese) in addition to Spanish, and have gained concessions from the Span-

Saint James the Great (Santiago in Spanish), Spain's patron saint, is intimately associated with the province of Galicia. When Galicians fought to maintain their independence during the Moorish occupation of Spain, the name of Santiago became their rallying cry.

ish government that allow the province a large degree of control over its own affairs.

During the Moorish conquest, Galicia also became a stronghold of the Catholic religion, having never been exposed to the influence of Islam, the faith of the invaders. Saint James the Great, one of the apostles of Christ and Spain's patron saint, has for centuries been associated with Galicia: legend has it that after his death, his followers placed his body in a boat, which drifted across the seas from Palestine to the coast of Galicia. The historic city of Santiago de Compostela, reportedly founded on the site of the apostle's grave, has attracted worshipers from all over the world since the Middle Ages.

Julio Iglesias (right), strolls with his parents and his younger brother, Carlos, during the late 1940s. Though Julio was determined to go his own way, Carlos later followed his father's footsteps and became a physician.

Though Julio did not become deeply religious, the age-old observances of Galicia remained with him throughout his life. "For me, tradition retains an enormous importance," he wrote. "In my house, we always pray before meals; afterward we bless the food that we have eaten, and I accept this not as a habit, not as a crutch, but because it is this, tradition."

Perhaps most important for a singer of romantic ballads, Julio was imbued at an early age with Galicia's rich and mysterious folklore. In addition to its strong religious faith, Galicia is a land that teems with myth and legend. The lonely stretches of rocky coastline and the dense, mist-shrouded forests have given rise to many strange visions through the centuries. Among the tales that abound to this day is that of the Santa Compañía, or Holy Company, a band of dead souls that wander the countryside at night, claiming the souls of the living. When they reach the house of a person marked for death, they announce their choice by throwing stones onto the roof. A living person who encounters these ghostly fiends can be saved only by drawing a circle on the ground and standing inside it or by clinging to a *cruceiro,* one of the many stone crucifixes that have been erected along the streets and roadways of Galicia. For the rest, Galician country people suggest countless ways of avoiding evil spells and ordinary bad luck: the remedies include avoiding the shade of walnut trees, taking care not to kill bees (which may embody the souls of deceased witches), and crossing the threshold of a house with the right foot only.

This atmosphere made such an impression on the young Julito, as his parents affectionately called him, that he later wrote of feeling himself to be something of a *meiga-brujo,* or warlock:

I believe there are things at my fingertips that I cannot manage or control. I recall vividly, with much pleasure and also a great deal of fear, the long walks I took with my father at twilight to Soto [a town near Cangas], sticking close to him as we walked along through little inlets echoing with strange sounds that seemed almost human—feeling a terror that still gives me gooseflesh. What memories I have of Galicia! How much it has influenced my music! ... It is not enough to say that the Galician tradition merely intrigues me; the point is that *I embody the Galician tradition.*

The foundation for his future art may have been built on these magical holidays, but for many years to come Julito's life was truly centered in Madrid. The Iglesias family, which included one other child, Julito's younger brother, Carlos, lived comfortably in the center of Madrid, near the spacious Parque del Oeste (Western Park). In later years, the man who had become an international heartthrob described himself as having been a "very ugly" child with a scrawny physique, a pale complexion, and hair that stuck up like barbed wire. At the same time, he was extremely sensitive, ready to laugh or cry over the smallest thing, and he felt a tremendous need to be the center of attention; normally, when he and his playmates got together, it was always Julio who organized the games they played, and chose the teams.

At the age of four, Julito began to attend the College of the Sacred Heart, a religious school located near his home. Though he behaved reasonably well, he was not a very good student. His mind was on soccer, the most popular sport throughout Spain, Europe, and much of the world. Even before he began to attend school, Julito had been able to see Sacred Heart's soccer field from the window of his room. He had been fascinated by the sights and sounds of the game, and by the age of six, he was a dedicated player. Unlike many youngsters, he did not dream of being a fleet-

Hungary's goalkeeper lunges to turn aside a shot during the 1954 World Cup final. As an up-and-coming soccer star, Iglesias developed a passion for playing goal: his desire to be the focus of attention later impelled him to pursue a career in show business.

footed forward with a booming shot. He wanted to play goal.

The goalkeeper was the ultimate performer, always in the spotlight. When he played poorly and let in goals, the spectators blamed him for losing the game. When he played brilliantly, on the other hand, the goalkeeper was the hero. That was all Julito desired: to have the ball in his hands, to be alone in the spotlight.

Julito loved soccer so much that he would even go to Sacred Heart during the vacations, just to play soccer with the priests. Though playing in their long black soutanes, the fathers—who came from areas such as Navarre and the Basque Provinces, famous for producing standout soccer players—were adept at the game. Perhaps to convince Julito of the need to spend more time with his books, they would put him in the goal and bombard him with blistering shots. However, the youngster always rose to the challenge. "Flying like an eagle from post to post," as he recalled, he turned aside shot after shot. The afternoons only succeeded in fueling his dream of hearing a packed soccer stadium ringing with cheers for him.

Julito was born at a time when many children in Spain were more concerned with having enough to eat than with starring on the soccer field. Between 1936 and 1939, Spain had been ravaged by civil war. The war began when a group of army officers rebelled against the workers' republic that had governed Spain since 1931. The rebels, led by General Francisco Franco, had the support of the army, the upper classes, and the church. The Republic, on the other hand, was defended by most of Spain's workers, by the labor unions, and by a variety of left-wing organizations that wished to change society.

As the fighting spread, the Spanish Civil War became a burning issue throughout Europe and North

Rescue workers sift through the rubble of an apartment building in Barcelona, Spain, after a March 7, 1939, bombing attack by Nationalist forces. The following month, Spain's three-year civil war ended with a Nationalist victory, leaving the nation battered and impoverished.

America. Germany and Italy, ruled by right-wing regimes, sent troops and modern weapons (especially airplanes) to aid the rebel cause. The Republic drew support from the International Brigades, groups of men and women who volunteered to fight in Spain, believing that the future of humanity depended on the outcome of the war. The defenders of the Republic, however, were no match for the disciplined and

heavily armed rebels—especially when the govern-
ments of Britain, France, and the United States refused
to aid the Republic's cause. By April 1939, Franco's
forces were in control of Spain, and Franco in-
stalled himself as the nation's dictator. More than
600,000 Spaniards died in the war; another 400,000
were executed by Franco, and 1 million more
were forced into exile.

*Spanish refugees, fleeing the advance of
Nationalist forces in April 1939, cross the
border into France. Though many Spaniards
struggled to survive during the decade
following the Spanish Civil War, the Iglesias
family lived securely and comfortably
in Madrid.*

The war left Spain on the verge of economic collapse, and the situation became even more dangerous in September 1939, when German troops invaded Poland and World War II began. In return for their help in the Civil War, the Germans urged Franco to join the Axis powers (Germany, Italy, and Japan) in declaring war on the Allies (Britain, France, and the Soviet Union). Franco was intelligent enough to real-

ize that Spain would be completely ruined by entry
into World War II. The nation's only hope of recovery
lay in remaining neutral and trying to secure financial
aid from both sides. Franco carried out this policy
with great skill throughout the war, but the supplies
he gained were far from adequate to meet the needs
of Spain's people during the war years. Spaniards of all
ages got used to going hungry, and many children had
their physical development impaired by a lack of
proper nutrition.

When the war ended in 1945 with the Axis
powers in ruins, Spain began a long and difficult
process of rebuilding its ties with the victors. Franco's
harsh methods of government and his sympathy for
the Axis powers made him an unpopular figure in the
postwar world. But gradually he convinced the government of the United States, now the leader of the
Western industrial nations, that Spain was a useful ally
against the Soviet Union, the nation that was now
regarded as a new threat to world peace. During the
1950s, the United States began to build air bases in
Spain. U.S. funds began to flow into the country, and
Spain's economic outlook brightened considerably.

For the Iglesias family, prosperous and respected,
these years could not have been more pleasant. All of
Julio's memories portray a secure and happy home life.
His respect and admiration for his father, a handsome,
dignified, studious man who devoted his life to a
noble profession, was boundless. His affection for his
mother ran no less deep. Because she was not obliged
to work outside the house, she was able to spend a
great deal of time with Julio and Carlos. The two boys
were close in age and were good friends, though they
competed with one another, as brothers will do. One
of their favorite contests was to see who had grown
more during the summer vacation. Each year, when
the family returned from Galicia to their house in

Madrid, the boys' mother would measure their height against a mark on the wall. Julio never forgot the sense of triumph he enjoyed upon learning that he had grown more than three inches taller during one summer, far outstripping his brother.

Oddly enough, the only real setback Julio encountered during his early years was a musical one. He had always responded to music as a child, picking out crude tunes on the family's piano and making up childish songs. He often used his small allowance to buy records—in those days thick, heavy 78 RPM discs made of shellac—featuring such popular performers of the day as Mina and Pedro Vargas. But when he finally tried to contribute his own musical talents to the Sacred Heart choir, he met with rejection. After hearing him sing, Father Anselmo, the choirmaster, remarked, "Tú al fútbol, que lo tuyo no es cantar." (Stick to soccer, singing is not your thing.) At the time, Julio was happy enough to follow that advice.

When he was finished with high school, Julio had to decide what to do with the rest of his life. His brother, Carlos, had already decided to follow in the footsteps of Dr. Iglesias and study medicine. Julio had his heart set on a soccer career, but he knew that he needed something else to fall back on. For that reason, he agreed to study law, which would make it possible for him to eventually obtain a post in the Spanish foreign ministry, leading to a comfortable life as a diplomat. He was diligently following this plan when he suffered the accident that redirected his energies toward the world of music.

C H A P T E R

T H R E E

"LA VIDA SIGUE IGUAL"

While he was recovering from his accident, Iglesias happened to watch a televised song festival with his mother. Watching the telecast, Iglesias jokingly told his mother that in a couple of years she would be seeing him at the festival. He had no idea that his idle thought would become reality. "If in 1966 you say to me I'm going to be a singer," he later told an interviewer, "I wouldn't believe it. Not ever. But people don't know what they have inside until they discover it one day."

Once he was recovered from his injuries, the immediate plan of the Iglesias family was for Julio to continue his law studies. There could be no more thought of starring as goalkeeper for Real Madrid, so he would have to concentrate on a more feasible career. Feeling that a change of scene would lift his son's spirits, Dr. Iglesias arranged for him to spend a year of study at Cambridge University in England.

Founded in the 13th century, Cambridge is one of the world's great universities. The university's exquisite buildings, most of them dating from the Middle Ages, stretch out along the river Cam in central England, surrounded by a countryside of farms and rolling hills. The months Julio spent in this peaceful setting remained a pleasant memory throughout his life, and long after his year at Cambridge he continued to wear a blue blazer bearing the university's crest. However, his months at Cambridge were not dominated by

Julio Iglesias, sporting the Cambridge University crest on his blazer, performs in Madrid in 1968. After trying out his songs on college audiences during his year of law studies at Cambridge, Iglesias returned to Spain with the dream of becoming an entertainer.

legal studies. Not long after his arrival, he met a young Frenchwoman, also an exchange student. The two young people began to spend a great deal of time together. Though Iglesias had come to Cambridge partly to increase his knowledge of English, he now found himself rapidly improving his French.

Iglesias had also brought his guitar with him, mostly as a diversion. Due to the inspiration of his French friend, he found himself composing love songs, and before long he was performing his songs in the pubs frequented by the Cambridge students. Feeling his strength and self-confidence returning after his long struggle against paralysis, he put the finishing touches on a song that he had begun during his convalescence in Madrid. Eventually entitled "La vida sigue igual" (Life Goes On), the song was to have an enormous influence on the rest of his career.

Iglesias returned to Spain in June 1967 in order to complete his law studies. However, his success as a performer in the Cambridge pubs had made a deep impression on him. The same desire for attention and recognition that had made him want to be a goalkeeper now impelled him toward a music career. He believed in his heart that he had the ability to be a successful entertainer. "When you are a young child," he later told an interviewer, "you dream about impossible things. When you are twenty years old, you start to dream with your eyes open." At the age of 24, Iglesias now knew what he wanted.

After all that he had put his parents through, it was difficult for him to tell them that he was thinking of abandoning a safe career for a venture as risky as songwriting. When he finally broached the subject, Dr. Iglesias came up with a sensible compromise: Julio would continue with his law studies but could spend his free time writing songs and trying to sell them, and his parents would give him all the help they could.

Cambridge University students relax along the river Cam, with King's College in the background. During his year at the prestigious British university, Iglesias spent much of his time with a French exchange student named Gwendolyne, who became his first true love.

This way, if he had no success in the music business, he would have a law degree to fall back on.

Spurred on by his parents' support, Iglesias began composing more songs and sending them to Spanish record companies. He used whatever connections he had to meet people in the music business, and he made sure that they took notice of him one way or another. Early in 1968, for example, he traveled to London to attend the annual Eurovision Song Festival, a popular television production in which singers and songwriters from all over Europe compete for prizes. At a party publicizing the event, he noticed the well-known Spanish songwriting team of Manuel de la Calva and Ramón Arcusa, who were known as the Dynamic Duo. Though the two men had no idea who Iglesias was, he approached them and introduced himself, telling them that he had heard their song performed during a rehearsal and was sure it would win first prize. He also told the songwriters that before the

end of the year they were going to see him performing. Both predictions came true.

Iglesias's brash assertion was based upon his growing self-confidence, not upon any genuine prospect
of being signed by a record company. Nevertheless,
as he continued to send out his songs, he gradually
caught the attention of executives at Discos Columbia, the Spanish-language division of the powerful
U.S. firm CBS Records. Discos Columbia's artistic
director, Linda Meredith, was not ready to buy any
of the young songwriter's work, but she encouraged
him to send in whatever he wrote. When she realized
how serious and determined Iglesias was, she also
invited him to come to her office and perform the
material himself.

After turning down many songs, Meredith finally
decided that one of Iglesias's efforts might have com-
mercial appeal, provided it was arranged and recorded
in the right way. She placed Iglesias in the hands of
two seasoned professionals: Enrique Garea, Discos
Columbia's A & R (artists and repertoire) manager,
and Augusto Alguero, the company's music director.
Between them, they chose one of the lines in the
song—"La vida sigue igual"—to serve as the title,
devised a musical arrangement, and hired a successful group called Los Gritos (The Shouts) to back up
Iglesias on the recording. After all this work was
done, Iglesias went into the studio to cut a demon-
stration record, or demo, the first step in any artist's
recording career.

Discos Columbia was so pleased with the demo
of "La vida sigue igual" that they proposed to enter
the song in that year's Benidorm Festival, one of
Spain's most important musical events.

Iglesias was delighted, but his father was becoming
worried. Julio had just received his law degree, and
Dr. Iglesias felt that it was time for his son to settle on

a career. After debating the subject, Julio and his father came to an agreement. If Julio's song won the Benidorm contest, which appeared highly unlikely, Dr. Iglesias would help him pursue a music career; if he did not win, Julio had to forget about songwriting and concentrate on law.

The festival, held at the popular resort city of Benidorm on Spain's Mediterranean coast, was scheduled for July 16–18, 1968. As the festival approached, the executives at Discos Columbia came up with a startling idea: they wanted Iglesias to perform "La vida sigue igual" himself.

The young songwriter was both flattered and frightened by the proposal. He objected that his only experience as a performer had come in Cambridge pubs; it was enough of an honor for him to have his song entered in the Benidorm Festival without pushing his luck. But the company had made up its mind. "Don't worry about it, kid," Enrique Garea told him. "Just go out and sing your song. Don't be nervous. Everything's going to be all right."

Iglesias was not convinced that things were going to be so easy. For one thing, he had to drive the 280 miles from Madrid to Benidorm in the fierce July heat, in a small car that overheated several times along the way. The only way he could keep the car from breaking down completely was to open the windows and drive with the heater on, venting heat from the engine into the saunalike passengers' compartment. He arrived in Benidorm in the early evening, registered at the hotel, and took a much-needed dip in the Mediterranean. When the contest officials informed Iglesias that he was scheduled to rehearse first thing in the morning, the news did nothing to calm his nerves.

The rehearsal took place in a local bullring; even though most of the seats were empty, there were

Iglesias's first record album,
Yo canto *(I Sing), was
released by Discos
Columbia at the end of
1968. Earlier in the year,
Iglesias had submitted
several songs to the record
company without success;
following his triumph at
the Benidorm Festival,
Columbia threw all its
weight behind him.*

enough spectators on hand to make Iglesias nervous—unlike most competitors, he had never sung
before so many people. To his relief, the rehearsal went
off without any mishaps. "At least no one threw
anything at me," he remarked as he left the stage.

Thirty-six hours later, on the evening of July 17,
the pressure was on. Now Iglesias had to perform
against competition, before a packed house. The night
was warm and humid—typical Mediterranean weath-
er. Wearing a white suit, Iglesias stood nervously in the
wings of the stage. Suddenly, he heard a voice ring out:
"First song: 'La vida sigue igual.' Words and music by
Julio Iglesias! Performed by the songwriter!"

That was Iglesias's cue to walk onstage, but he was
so nervous that his legs simply refused to move. Finally,
Enrique Garea took hold of him and gave him a firm
push that propelled him, half stumbling, onto the
stage. All he could remember afterward was that he

had his hands jammed into his pockets as he stood before the audience, a strange beginning for a singer who was later noted for his expressive gestures on-stage. The music began—as he later recalled, "I drew my voice from the depths of my soul and sang."

Indeed, "La vida sigue igual" was more than just a song for Iglesias. The words and the music expressed the ordeal he had suffered after his accident and the inner strength that had enabled him to get back on his feet and take his life in a new direction. He had accepted the risks that a full life demands, the knowledge that men and women truly have a short time on earth, that friendships and relationships often fade away. Nevertheless, the lyrics insist, one must have something worth struggling for, someone to love—because in the end, whatever happens for good or ill, life does go on.

And then the song was over. People were applauding. Iglesias went back to the wings, where his friends embraced him and told him he had done well. He had survived the first step, and after all the songs had been heard, the judges included Iglesias in a group of 10 finalists slated to compete for the first prize on the following day.

The second time around, Iglesias was scheduled to sing ninth. His nerves were now completely under control; more than anything, he felt a determination to succeed. As he prepared to go on, he thought, This is my opportunity. Don't let it go by. This is my moment.

Once again, Iglesias sang "La vida sigue igual" with all his inner conviction. Two hours later, he recalled, he was in a daze, "stuck in a corner like a plant," being interviewed for the Spanish national television network. He had won the first prize at Benidorm, and his life was changed forever.

The Beatles in the mid-1960s. For the recording of Iglesias's first album, Discos Columbia hired London's Decca Studios, where the British rockers had cut some of their early records—the company hoped that the phenomenal success of the Beatles would rub off on the young Spaniard.

GWENDOLYNE AND ISABEL

By winning first prize at the Benidorm Festival, Iglesias was transformed overnight from an unknown songwriter to a rising star. There was no longer any debate at home about the possibility of a diplomatic career. Julio was free to pursue his music wholeheartedly.

Discos Columbia was equally enthusiastic. As soon as Iglesias put his signature to a recording contract, the company's publicists sprang into action, distributing photos of Iglesias and biographical handouts to all the newspapers and magazines in Spain. Meanwhile, the production staff went all out to release a studio recording of "La vida sigue igual" in the shortest possible time. The record was in the stores by September, and within two weeks it had reached the top of the charts in Spain.

The spectacular success of the single record convinced Discos Columbia that Iglesias was ready to record a complete album. As a way of showing their belief in the young singer, and in an attempt to bring him luck, the company arranged for him to record the album at the Decca Studios in London. Decca Studios possessed some of the most advanced recording technology then available anywhere in the world, and they had also gained a powerful mystique in the music industry. The Beatles, then at the height of their world-wide popularity, had recorded a number of records in the same studios Iglesias was preparing to use.

The album Iglesias recorded in London was enti-tled *Yo canto* (I Sing). Released in late 1968, *Yo canto* featured "La vida sigue igual" and 11 other songs that Iglesias had written at Cambridge—the very same songs that he had tried to sell to Discos Columbia without success, before his Benidorm triumph. Now the company was so eager to market their new talent that they scheduled a second album—*Todos los días un día* (Every Day Is the Same)—for early 1969, even though Iglesias had not yet had time to compose a new batch of songs. Discos Columbia solved this problem by teaming Iglesias up with other songwrit-ers, notably Manuel de la Calva and Ramón Arcusa. The Dynamic Duo had not forgotten their meeting with Iglesias during the previous year, nor his confi-dent prediction that they would be hearing about him in the near future.

Initially impressed by the young singer's ambition and talent, Arcusa and de la Calva were now equally struck by his capacity for hard work and his attention to detail. As de la Calva told an interviewer after several years of working with Iglesias: "He's a born worker. He is a perfectionist. He looks for perfection beyond anyone's understanding. There is always a bet-ter interpretation of a phrase, and he searches for it. No matter what he has done, he wants more. Every-one can say it's fantastic, but still he'll want to repeat and repeat and repeat until he finds the interpretation, precision, and sentiment he wants to give each word."

The release of the album touched off a campaign to provide maximum exposure for Iglesias in Spain. Discos Columbia arranged a concert tour cover-ing all the nation's major cities. At each stop, Iglesias launched into a new batch of newspaper and magazine interviews and appearances on local radio shows. He found the grueling schedule to his liking. "I like people," he told an interviewer who wondered how he was handling all the demands on his time. "Perhaps other artists don't enjoy being surrounded by people, but I do."

The public appeared to return the young singer's affection. In addition to enjoying Iglesias's music, looks, and personality, people were intrigued and touched by accounts of his injury, recovery, and sudden success as a performer. The dramatic story had such appeal that Iglesias signed a contract to play himself in a motion picture, not surprisingly entitled *La vida sigue igual*.

For an artist possessed with Iglesias's drive, a hit single, a successful album, and a tour of Spain were nothing more than warm-ups. Both Iglesias and Discos Columbia knew that the music market in Spain, a nation of 38 million people, was in reality a rather limited one. There was a whole world outside of Spain, and Iglesias was determined to conquer it.

The first step, logically, was to go after the Spanish-speaking population abroad, specifically in the huge continent of South America, where some 250 million people enjoyed a variety of rich musical traditions, ranging from native Indian music to popular tunes from Europe and the United States. Seeking to tap this lucrative market, Discos Columbia entered Iglesias in the song contest at Viña del Mar, Chile. Held annually in the beautiful resort on the Pacific Ocean, the Viña del Mar Festival was as important in South America as Benidorm was in Spain.

The festival was a triumph for Iglesias. He fell in love with Viña del Mar, returning there often during the following years. The Chileans in the audience, known to be harsh with lackluster performers, gave the young Spaniard a warm reception. He also had the

*The Argentine tango singer Carlos Gardel, photographed during a 1930s radio broadcast.
Following Iglesias's early success in Spain, the young Spaniard set his sights on conquering
Latin America, where a large population of Spanish speakers enjoyed a rich musical heritage
built around such legendary performers as Gardel.*

opportunity to meet several important figures in the South American music world; by the time the festival ended, Iglesias had laid the foundation for his future popularity in Chile and the rest of South America.

While in the Americas, Iglesias also established a tradition that was to continue throughout his career by making himself available for charity events. In this case, he accepted an invitation from the International Red Cross to sing at a benefit for earthquake victims in the Central American nation of Guatemala. Returning to Europe at the end of 1969, Iglesias finished his whirlwind year by appearing at the San Remo Festival on the Italian Riviera.

In 1970, Iglesias truly began to emerge as a force on the European musical scene. He began the year by performing at a music industry convention in Cannes, France, and in February, he took part in a music festival in Barcelona, Spain. The Barcelona event had a special significance because the winner of the competition would represent Spain in the 1970 Eurovision Song Festival, to be held in Amsterdam, Holland. Iglesias prepared for Barcelona with his usual care and energy; in addition to winning first prize, he had the pleasure of seeing his father in the audience. Completely reconciled to Julio's musical career, the elegant and dignified physician made no attempt to hide his excitement. According to Elizabeth García in her book *Julio,* Dr. Iglesias predicted to everyone within earshot that his son was going to be the next Frank Sinatra. (If record sales are taken as a criterion, Iglesias went on to surpass the American superstar's popularity by a wide margin.)

The Eurovision Song Festival—broadcast to 24 countries, with a total viewing audience of 400 million—became a major turning point for Iglesias. Though he finished in fourth place, most of those who attended the festival felt that the song he performed, "Gwendolyne," had been the best in the contest but that other songs had appealed more to the judges for one reason or another. Certainly, the song had the most personal meaning for Iglesias than any he had ever written. "La vida sigue igual" had expressed his acceptance of life's challenges; "Gwendolyne" sprang directly from his emotions.

The song was, purely and simply, a tribute to Iglesias's first real love, the French exchange student he had met during his year at Cambridge. For Iglesias, the encounter with Gwendolyne had a double significance: it was not only a source of emotional enrichment, as all genuine love affairs are; it was also a reentry into the world for a young man who had so recently faced the prospect of lifelong paralysis. Writing his autobiography nearly 20 years later, he still spoke of Gwendolyne with unashamed sentiment and romanticism: "Broad cheekbones, blonde hair, steel-gray eyes. . . . I have to say something that is burning inside me: she has been, and still is, the most beautiful woman in my life. . . . At times her memory scorches me, with tremendous power, as though I held a live coal in my hand."

Iglesias expressed all these emotions in "Gwendolyne," describing the way in which a powerful romantic attachment can survive both the passage of time and the experience of other loves. Though the Eurovision judges placed three songs ahead of "Gwendolyne," the public quickly rendered its own verdict. Iglesias's recording of the song became the best-selling disc of 1970, in both Europe and Latin America. The 27-year-old Spaniard was now established as an international star.

Typically, Iglesias's breakthrough into a wider market only increased his passion for work. Returning to Spain from Amsterdam, he embarked on a monthlong concert tour that involved a staggering

Sophie Garel and Chris Bala of Luxembourg perform at the 1968 Eurovision Song Festival. The following year, Iglesias made the festival a personal showcase. Though his song "Gwendolyne" failed to win the first prize, it received exposure that soon made it the number one record throughout the Continent.

total of 41 concerts, in 41 different cities. Then he flew to Japan, where he performed at a festival in the city of Osaka. While all this activity was taking place, he managed to record two complete albums, *Soy* (I Am) and *Gwendolyne.* Perhaps even more important, he also fell in love.

Iglesias's obsession with his career had caused him to put off any thoughts about settling down, but it had never blinded him to the other aspects of life. He was often seen in the company of attractive women, and as his stature as a performer grew, he became friendly with some of the leading personalities on the international social circuit. Having made fans of such luminaries as Princess Grace of Monaco and the Aga Khan, Iglesias was a frequent guest at lavish social events, both in Spain and abroad.

In May 1970, Iglesias attended a party in Madrid honoring a well-known Spanish dancer, Manuela Vargas. It was just the sort of party Iglesias most enjoyed, attended by "everyone who was anyone" in Madrid, including many members of the so-called jet set. During the festivities, Iglesias noticed a delicate, dark-haired woman and was captivated, as he recalled, by "her skin, her big, mysterious eyes, her tremendous sense of style."

Iglesias asked the host of the party, his friend Juan Olmedilla, who she was. Olmedilla revealed that the woman's name was Isabel Preysler and that she belonged to a wealthy family in the Philippines. (The Philippines, an island nation in the Pacific Ocean, was once a Spanish colony; though long independent, the Philippines still maintains close ties with Spain, and Spanish remains an official language of the nation.) Only 17 years old, Preysler had come to Madrid to study and also to meet people at the upper levels of Spanish society. Iglesias asked Olmedilla to introduce him to Preysler during the course of the evening, but with all the activity taking place at the party, the introduction never occurred.

Two weeks later, Olmedilla phoned Iglesias and invited him to another glamorous party taking place in Madrid that weekend. Iglesias said that he was not planning to be in town. He had been spending his weekends in London, where he was recording another album at Decca Studios, and he was also dating an English actress, Jane Harrington, who had appeared with him in the film *La vida sigue igual*. Shortly after he spoke with Olmedilla, Iglesias received a call from another friend, Julio Ayesa. Ayesa said that Iglesias should come to the party because a woman who interested him was going to be there. Iglesias replied that almost all the women he met interested him—he still had plans for the weekend. But when he learned that the woman in question was Isabel Preysler, his response was instantaneous: "Count on me— I'll be there."

This time, Preysler and Iglesias were formally introduced. She did not appear to be overly impressed by his growing reputation as an international singing star, and this actually pleased him. At the end of the evening, he asked Preysler for her telephone number. She replied that there was no point in his having her number because she was about to return to the Philippines for a vacation. Iglesias believed that she was just trying to put him off. He decided to "make a nuisance" of himself until Preysler either agreed to see him or told him point-blank to leave her alone. From a mutual friend, he obtained her phone number and called her from London. Surprised by the call, Preysler agreed to go out with Iglesias when he returned to Madrid.

On their first date, Iglesias and Preysler attended a concert, had a casual dinner, and then went dancing at a popular club. They saw each other the following day, and the day after that, and the day after that. Iglesias was aware that Preysler liked him, but he also knew that she was, as he recalled, "skeptical" about their relationship. For his own part, he was completely captivated by the beautiful teenager. He felt that she was different from the women he had been dating, and there was no question in his mind of simply engaging in a fleeting love affair with Preysler. After realizing that he was in no position to marry his first love, Gwendolyne, he had never even considered the idea of marriage again. But after several dates with Preysler, he said to himself, This is the woman of my life. I am going to marry her.

The courtship was not a particularly smooth one because of the tremendous demands of Iglesias's schedule. Whenever he had a free moment, he hopped on a plane or a train and hurried off to the town of Guardamar on the Mediterranean, where Preysler was spending the summer. In the fall, Iglesias embarked on another tour of Latin America, and he phoned every day from wherever he happened to be performing. Finally, he recalled, "with my voice much steadier than

Dr. Julio Iglesias Puga kisses his new granddaughter, Chaveli, as the child's mother, Isabel Preysler de Iglesias, looks on. Though Chaveli's father was present for her birth, he was soon off on another singing engagement.

my legs," he stated during one call, "Isabel, why don't we get married? We should get married." Preysler turned him down.

In December, when Iglesias was back in Spain, he repeated the proposal in person. This time, Preysler accepted. She and Iglesias were married in the historic city of Toledo on January 20, 1971. After a honeymoon in the Canary Islands, a Spanish possession off the coast of North Africa, they settled in a small rented house in Madrid and began their life together. Before the year was over, Iglesias's album sales had passed 1 million, and he was the father of a baby girl, Chaveli. He appeared truly blessed, but there was much hard work and more than a little disappointment ahead.

JULIO IGLESIAS
EL AMOR

CBS

50306

CONQUERING THE WORLD

The cover of Iglesias's 1975 album El amor (Love) *conveys the romantic appeal he exerted on female fans throughout the world. At this point in his career, Iglesias was truly an international star, with record sales in the tens of millions.*

Iglesias began 1972 by recording one of his most heartfelt and memorable songs, "Un canto a Galicia" (A Song for Galicia). The song was at the same time a tribute to his father's heritage, a celebration of his own childhood memories, and a branching out into new directions. The greatest novelty in the recording was Iglesias's use of the Galician language: he sang the first four verses in Galician, and then repeated them in Spanish. According to Elizabeth García, some Galicians—extremely protective of their distinctive culture—complained that Iglesias had failed to correctly pronounce all the words in the song. Apart from that, "Un canto a Galicia" was a colossal hit, not only in Spain but throughout Europe. The song also reached the top of the charts in Latin America, where many Galicians had settled over the years, and its phenomenal popularity even spread to North Africa and the Middle East. Both the music and the lyrics conveyed the Galician sense of *morriña,* roughly translated as "the blues," which is specifically associated with longing or nostalgia for one's homeland. Thus, the song actually had an appeal that cut across borders and language barriers, striking a chord with anyone who felt an attachment for something no longer within reach.

"Un canto a Galicia" also indicated a growing trend in the way Discos Columbia was marketing Iglesias. The company had decided that he had the potential to be a worldwide attraction. This being the case, there was no reason why he should make records exclusively in Spanish. He was able to speak French, German, Italian, and English well enough to put his songs across in those languages. He released his first album in German in 1972, and the German public received it with enthusiasm. Discos Columbia executive Gerhard Haltermann, quoted by Elizabeth García, described Iglesias's impact on a German audience during a live performance: "The audience honestly believed that he understood and felt every word that he was singing. Of course, his pronunciation when done live wasn't always perfect, yet at the exact moment, he would give just the right intonation. They loved it when he sang the word 'heart' in German. Everyone would go wild because they genuinely felt he knew exactly what he was saying."

As Iglesias's worldwide record sales mounted into the millions, his lifestyle began to reflect his ever-increasing income. He had already established a spacious home in Madrid, and now he began to invest in real estate all over the world. He bought a house on the island of Majorca in the Mediterranean, a ranch in Argentina, and another vacation home on the South Pacific island of Tahiti.

Throughout his career, Iglesias proved to be an energetic and shrewd businessman as well as a hard-working performer. He enjoyed meeting prominent figures in the business world and paid close attention to the financial aspects of his performing career. Working in a business in which many popular performers had traditionally been exploited by promoters and managers, Iglesias made sure that he got his fair share of all the money he generated, not only in record sales but in the proceeds from concerts, television appearances, and product endorsements. Though he had once chafed at his father's insistence that he obtain his law degree, he was now grateful for the expertise he had gained. "I'm probably the only singer in the world who understands the fine print in his contract," he told an interviewer.

Iglesias's family was growing along with his career. His first son, also named Julio José, was born in 1973, and Enrique followed in 1975. Iglesias was at his wife's side during the birth of both boys, but in general, he maintained such a hectic performing schedule that he was rarely able to spend much time at home. During the course of 1973, he was on the road almost con-

Iglesias enjoys an outing at Miami's Seaquarium with his three children, (left to right) Chaveli, Julio José, and Enrique. Though deeply attached to his wife and children, Iglesias always admitted that he lived for his career. "The challenges that I have professionally always come first," he said.

tinually, touring Europe, Latin America, and selected
cities in the United States with large Hispanic popu-
lations. The more he succeeded, the more obsessed
he was with topping what he had already achieved.
Alfredo Capalgo, an Argentine promoter, described
for Elizabeth García Iglesias's determination to capti-
vate the citizens of Buenos Aires, Argentina's capital:

> There's a street in Buenos Aires . . . called
> Florida. The street is primarily made up of
> movie houses. It's always crowded with people.
> One day Julio asked me to take him there, to see
> if anyone would recognize him. We went to the
> street, and no one gave him a second glance.
> Julio thought about it and told me that he'd only
> be important the day he could walk down Flor-
> ida Street and everyone would know him. On
> his third trip to Buenos Aires, he asked me to
> take him back to Florida Street. It was amazing.
> It was impossible for him to get near it. He had
> become their idol.

Having conquered Europe and Latin America,
Iglesias then began to focus on the greatest challenge
of all: the vast and lucrative music market in the
United States. It was a market unmatched by any in
the world, providing scope for performers as varied as
romantic crooners, country singers, folk balladeers,
and heavy-metal thrashers, so there should have been
a generous niche for Iglesias. But as Marsha Daley
points out in her 1986 book *Julio Iglesias,* "Non-
English-speaking entertainers have never succeeded
on a superstar level in America. Several Latin and
Gallic celebrities had been promoted in years past, but
aside from a fleeting sensation caused by Maurice
Chevalier in the 1930s, most had been relegated to
second billing—Xavier Cugat, Carmen Miranda,
and, unless supported by his superstar wife Lucille
Ball, Desi Arnaz, among others. Except for the
British, Americans were not very receptive to for-

eign accents. Even supersexy Yves Montand had never been able to penetrate the American heartland with his French songs."

Iglesias was determined to succeed where others had failed, and Discos Columbia was prepared to back him by sponsoring a 1974 concert in New York City. However, the project suffered a setback when Iglesias unintentionally offended an important segment of the Hispanic population in the United States. He was performing at a nightclub in Miami, Florida, a city that had become a second home for many Cubans who had left their native island after Fidel Castro's Communist revolution in 1958. Most Miami Cubans were vehemently anti-Communist and anti-Castro and would not tolerate anyone who approved of Castro or his government. During his act, Iglesias chatted with the audience; realizing that there were a number of Cubans present, he remarked that he would also like to sing for those who were still living on the island of Cuba. He meant this purely as a statement of his affection for all Cubans, but some members of the audience took it as a gesture of support for Castro (who was, incidentally, said to be a big fan of Iglesias's). One man threw a glass at the stage, and a near riot ensued. In the aftermath, Iglesias's records were banned from Spanish-language radio stations in Miami and other cities having a large Cuban exile population. Some of the more violent anti-Castro elements even threatened to kill Iglesias if he ever set foot in the United States again.

Despite the threats, Discos Columbia was determined to go ahead with the concert plans. They booked an afternoon date for Iglesias in New York's historic Carnegie Hall; following this event, he was to fly to Miami for an evening concert designed to win back his Cuban-American following. The promoters took the death threats against Iglesias quite seriously

Iglesias performs at a sold-out concert at New York's Radio City Music Hall. Beginning with his triumphant appearance at Carnegie Hall in 1976, Iglesias demonstrated his ability to attract a mass audience in the United States, a feat that no previous foreign singer had been able to accomplish.

and made extensive security arrangements, which included the presence of dogs trained to sniff out explosives.

As the concert progressed, it became apparent that there was no need to worry about Iglesias's safety or his appeal to the New York audience. As Elizabeth García described the event, "Julio sang accompanied by twenty-eight of New York's finest musicians. . . . Besides singing in Spanish, he sang in Galician, French, Italian, and even ventured into English. . . . By the show's end, he had the audience on its feet, yelling bravo and urging him to do encore after encore." Finally, Iglesias had to tear himself away, rush to the airport with a police escort, and catch a plane for Miami. His performance there was greeted with the same enthusiasm, and the following day, his records were being heard on Spanish-language radio stations once again.

Iglesias's success at Carnegie Hall gained him a foothold in the U.S. market, and in 1976, Discos Columbia decided that the time had come for an even bigger New York concert. This time the venue would be Madison Square Garden, the ultimate arena for pop music performers. The concert followed the release of three more highly successful and diversified albums. *El amor* (Love), which featured former Beatle George Harrison's "My Sweet Lord" as well as a half dozen new tunes by Iglesias, had been another spectacular success worldwide, selling 500,000 copies in France alone. In *A México* and *América,* Iglesias directly courted Spanish-speaking listeners in the New World, singing a variety of traditional and modern songs from Mexico, Cuba, and other Latin American nations: "María bonita," "Guantanamera," "Vaya con Dios," and "Júrame," among others. The effect on his popularity among Spanish speakers in the United States was immediately apparent when his Madison Square

Garden concert broke all previous box-office records
for the arena. Iglesias fans turned out in force, and not
only from the New York City area; quite a number
traveled from cities as distant as Philadelphia and
Washington, D.C.

In 1977, Iglesias broke another record when more
than 100,000 Chileans turned out to hear him perform at the National Stadium in Santiago, Chile's
capital. During the course of the year, *El amor* became
the top-selling album in Europe, Latin America,
Canada, the Middle East, and Africa, in addition to
enjoying healthy sales in the United States and Asia.
The same level of success greeted *A mis 33 años*
(My 33 Years), which featured a number of new
songs by Iglesias's favorite collaborators, Manuel de
la Calva and Ramón Arcusa.

Iglesias's impact on the pop music scene now
covered such a broad spectrum that he shifted from
Discos Columbia to another CBS label, CBS International, which provided a more extensive worldwide marketing approach. Under CBS International's
direction, he recorded his first albums in French
and Italian. As a result, he won artist of the year
awards in both France and Italy, as well as in several
other countries.

While Iglesias was branching out into countless
new areas, Spain itself was changing rapidly. In 1975,
Francisco Franco, who had ruled as the nation's dictator since the end of the Spanish Civil War in 1939,
died at the age of 84. Under Franco, Spain had existed
in a state of political and spiritual isolation. While
other Western Europeans enjoyed democratic government and the free exchange of ideas, Spaniards lived
under the iron rule of Franco and his Falangist party.
Elections were a sham, as all political parties opposed
to the government were outlawed. The Cortes, Spain's
parliament, had little power of its own. Books, news-

papers, films, radio, and television were all strictly censored by the government and the Catholic church. Many of Spain's greatest artists, such as the painter Pablo Picasso, the musician Pablo Casals, and the filmmaker Luis Buñuel, had refused to set foot on Spanish soil as long as Franco remained in power; their indignation was shared by most enlightened people throughout the world and by many ordinary Spaniards, especially among the younger generation.

Franco's death released the spirit and energy that had been lying dormant in the Spanish nation. As early as 1969, Franco had decreed that the Spanish monarchy, suspended since 1931, would resume after his death. He designated as his successor Prince Juan Carlos de Borbón, the grandson of King Alfonso XIII, expecting that Juan Carlos would seek to carry on the

King Juan Carlos I and Queen Sofía of Spain attend a special mass celebrating the king's swearing-in as head of state in November 1975. Under the enlightened reign of Juan Carlos, Spain has become a democratic nation and a respected member of the world community.

tradition of extreme right-wing government. Fortunately for Spain, after the prince ascended the throne as King Juan Carlos I, he proved to be an intelligent and forward-looking leader. Realizing that Spain needed to rejoin the community of free nations, Juan Carlos supported free elections and a genuine decision-making role for the Cortes. In 1977, the Spanish government acceded to the king's demands. When the regime lifted the ban on political parties and took the

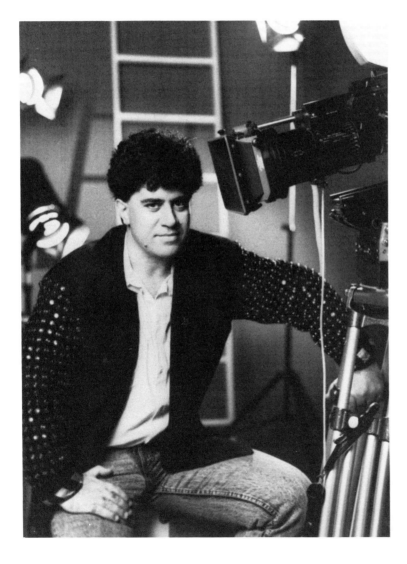

Pedro Almodóvar, the director of such offbeat films as Women on the Verge of a Nervous Breakdown, *exemplifies the artistic revolution in contemporary Spain, where experimental forms of art have cut into the popularity of traditional performers such as Iglesias.*

first steps toward a democratic constitution, Spain entered a new phase of its history.

Along with its political resurgence, Spain experienced an explosion in the field of the arts. Free of all government interference, Spanish painters, writers, musicians, and filmmakers gave free rein to their creative impulses. Many works looked back critically at the Franco years, while others celebrated the challenges of modern life. Perhaps the most successful of this new artistic generation was the young filmmaker Pedro Almodóvar, whose outrageous, sexually liberated comedies would have been unthinkable under the Franco regime.

In this new atmosphere, more traditional performers such as Iglesias were at a disadvantage. In addition, Iglesias came in for a certain amount of criticism from people who had suffered under the Franco regime. The Iglesias family had long been linked with the Spanish establishment, and Julio himself had been friendly with Franco's grandsons when he was growing up. (In his autobiography, Iglesias denied that he ever received any favors from the Francos and asserted that his political views had always been more liberal than conservative.) As his popularity in Spain declined somewhat, he had reason to be pleased with the efforts he had made to build up a worldwide following. He did not yet realize that the time and effort he was expending on his career was gradually destroying his home life.

CHAPTER
SIX

"THE NEW
VALENTINO"

By the time he signed with CBS International in 1978, Iglesias was more than an international singing star. He had become a romantic figure who exerted an unusual brand of fascination. In the world of show business, there are at any given moment a handful of male singers and actors who enjoy a wide romantic appeal. During the 1970s, the British singer Tom Jones often rivaled Iglesias in popularity with female audiences. However, the two singers were completely different onstage. Jones, a muscular, curly-haired Welshman, was a rough-and-ready, high-energy performer who usually finished his act drenched with perspiration, with his shirt unbuttoned and his hair tousled. Iglesias, on the other hand, always maintained an aura of suave elegance. He opened his act alone on a darkened stage, illuminated by a single spotlight, always formally dressed in a tuxedo. Though his singing style was often intense and emotional, he communicated purely through his voice, his facial expressions, and his trademark mannerism of pressing his right hand to his heart or his stomach as though he were trying desperately to contain the explosive power of his romantic longing. The effect was no less electrifying than Jones's gyrations. A reporter covering Iglesias's record-breaking Madison Square Garden concert noted that many of the women in the audience

Iglesias entertains an overflow audience at Paris's Palais du Congrès in 1981. At this point in his career, Iglesias was being touted as an international sex symbol. "I'm a very normal guy," he explained. "But if I represent something when I go on the stage and the people love it, I think it's great."

"swooned, whistled, made suggestive gestures, blew kisses, and threw roses at their idol."

Iglesias's impact was such that the press began to refer to him as "the new Valentino." They were refer-ring to the worldwide upheaval generated during the 1920s by the silent-film star Rudolph Valentino. The Italian-born Valentino, who began his career as a dancer and movie extra, achieved phenomenal popu-larity when he starred in such early films as *The Sheik, Blood and Sand,* and *Monsieur Beaucaire.* Film historian Ephraim Katz has described Valentino's effect in the following terms: "To the American woman he repre-sented a symbol of mysterious, forbidden eroticism, a vicarious fulfillment of dreams of illicit love and unin-hibited passions." Valentino's sudden death at the age of 31, in 1926, achieved the status of a major calamity. "Thousands of women lined the streets during his funeral," Katz writes, "causing a near riot. . . . Years after his death, Valentino fan clubs around the country were as active in glorifying their hero as they had been during the peak of his career. Every year on the anniversary of his death, a mysterious woman in black has been seen laying a wreath of flowers on his grave, adding a sense of drama to the life and death of a screen legend."

Becoming the successor of a man who had aroused such emotion was clearly a major accom-plishment, but it was not easy to reconcile the image of "the new Valentino" with the reality of being a husband and father. During the first year of Iglesias's marriage to Isabel Preysler, Preysler had played an active and essential role in his career. She had traveled with him to all his performance dates, supervising many of the arrangements herself. It became immedi-ately clear that Preysler was as much a perfectionist as her husband, and her support and advice had helped him define his approach to his art.

Rudolph Valentino, shown here in a scene from the 1922 silent film Blood and Sand, *had an electrifying effect on female moviegoers. As Julio Iglesias began to emerge as an international heartthrob, the media quickly dubbed him "the new Valentino."*

Once the Iglesiases became parents, however, Preysler was obliged to adopt a different role. She remained in Madrid with the children, waiting for her husband to return from recording sessions and far-flung performance tours. In itself, this promised to be difficult for an intelligent, energetic woman who had originally come to Madrid with the idea of establishing a career and achieving her own place in society. The situation could only be complicated by Iglesias's image as the world's foremost heartthrob; everywhere he went, Iglesias was reportedly being pursued by women, and at least according to the gossip columnists, he did not always run away. These were not ideal conditions under which to maintain a successful marriage.

The couple also found that for all their mutual affection, there were serious differences between their personalities. As Iglesias noted in his autobiography, his "Spanish vehemence" caused him to be extremely vocal whenever he was displeased about something. Preysler, on the other hand, following what he termed her "Oriental pragmatism," met his outbursts with a dignified silence. As a result, Iglesias believed, he and Preysler were never able to discuss their problems and look for solutions. They could only continue to pursue their own lives, each partner feeling misunderstood and unfairly treated by the other. Iglesias realized that he was always devoting more energy to his career than to his family, but he was neither willing nor able to change. He had committed himself to his work, and he felt bound to pursue it with fanatical devotion. By 1979, after seven years together, Iglesias and Preysler decided that they could no longer remain married.

The couple carried out their decision to separate very quickly, but the effects of the breakup lingered with Iglesias for a long time. Even after several years had passed, he was not ashamed to admit that he was still very attached to Preysler and was deeply disappointed that their marriage had failed. Preysler herself was eventually to remarry, have another child, and begin a highly successful career as a journalist and television personality.

Iglesias stated his intention never to remarry, and he devoted himself to his career with renewed passion. "I almost went crazy," he admitted. "Crazy to forget everything that had happened." His way of dulling the emotional pain he felt was to travel from city to city at a frenetic pace, to spend hour after hour working on a single phrase in a song.

Iglesias also decided that it was a time for him to make a break with the past by relocating his main residence. Because he was more determined than ever to make a serious impact on the U.S. market, it made sense for him to live in the United States, where he could travel more easily to concert dates and be available for interviews and television appearances. With this in mind, he purchased a mansion in the Miami area, in a secluded and exclusive community named Indian Creek. He threw himself into redecorating the house, which features three swimming

In 1979, Iglesias left Madrid and acquired this spacious mansion in Indian Creek, an exclusive community in Miami, Florida. The move provided a needed change of scene after the breakup of Iglesias's marriage and also made it easier for the singer to break into the U.S. market.

pools and a private dock for Iglesias's three yachts. The singer's decision to move away from Spain, combined with his luxurious way of life, drew criticism in the Spanish press. Iglesias's detractors charged that he was leaving Spain because the voters had elected a socialist government, which was expected to raise taxes on the rich in order to provide greater benefits for Spain's working people. Iglesias hotly denied these charges, reaffirming his allegiance to Spain, his liberal political sentiments, and his record of faithfully paying his Spanish income taxes.

Now that he was officially a single man again, Iglesias's role as an international sex symbol became even more sharply defined. As a measure of his celebrity status and his reputation as a connoisseur of women, he was invited to serve as one of the judges at the 1979 Miss Universe pageant, held in Australia. The contest provided a welcome diversion from Iglesias's grueling touring schedule, which once again covered Europe, Latin America, the Middle East, and North America.

In 1979, Iglesias released another major album, *Emociones* (Emotions). The album drew heavily upon the contributions of Manuel de la Calva and Ramón Arcusa, with whom Iglesias now shared both a long-standing professional partnership and a growing personal bond. One of the more interesting aspects of the album was Iglesias's excursion into the world of opera: along with de la Calva and Arcusa, he adapted the haunting Polovetsian dances from Nikolai Borodin's *Prince Igor* into a love song entitled "Quiéreme" (Love Me). The public's response to the album rewarded the renewed effort that Iglesias was putting into his career, as sales figures broke all the records set by his previous releases.

As a new decade began, Iglesias had unquestionably secured a place in the front rank of international superstars. In 1980, President Anwar Sadat of Egypt invited Iglesias to perform in a spectacular outdoor concert outside Cairo, with the floodlit pyramids as a backdrop. The following year, he traveled to the tiny but highly fashionable European principality of Monaco, at the invitation of Princess Grace, to perform at a ball benefiting the International Red Cross. When his album *Hey* was released in 1980, it rocketed to the top of the charts in more than 80 countries.

While touring and recording, Iglesias was also keeping the gossip columnists busy, as always. He was often seen in the company of a glamorous actress named Sidney Rome, who was also experiencing the breakup of a marriage, and he did not deny that they were in love. The romance lasted a year, and as Iglesias stated in his autobiography, "It left a sweet taste in my mouth." In the case of Priscilla Presley, however,

Plainclothes police officers surround the wreckage of a bombed military car on a busy Madrid street in 1981. The bombing, which took the lives of three army officers and wounded the king's top military adviser, was the work of Basque terrorists.

Iglesias was less forthcoming. He met Elvis Presley's widow—then embarking on her own career as a singer and actress—at the Viña del Mar Festival in 1981; though he saw Presley frequently after that meeting, he continued to insist that they were merely friends.

At the same time, however, Iglesias learned that being a worldwide celebrity could have a dark and terrifying underside. This truth had been brought home in shocking fashion in December 1980, when pop star John Lennon was shot to death outside his Manhattan apartment building by a demented fan. Following this event, many music and film stars sought to ensure their personal safety by hiring bodyguards and adopting other security measures. Iglesias thought about hiring protection, but finally decided not to do so. Perhaps he decided that there was no way for a public personality to be completely invulnerable. When the assault came, it arose from a source that neither he nor anyone else could have anticipated.

On December 29, 1981, Dr. Julio Iglesias Puga was kidnapped in Madrid. Several days earlier, he had been contacted by two men claiming to be from South America; the men said that they were journalists who had been assigned by a German magazine to interview the doctor. After a number of discussions, Dr. Iglesias agreed to the interview, saying that he would meet with the supposed journalists shortly after New Year's Day, which he was planning to spend in Miami with his son. The kidnappers decided not to wait; they accosted the doctor outside his clinic, forced him into a car at gunpoint, and hustled him out of Madrid.

Shortly after the kidnapping, the deeply shaken Iglesias family was informed that the kidnappers had demanded ransom in the amount of $2 million, half in U.S. dollars and half in Spanish pesetas. At first, the

*Carlos Iglesias speaks on
the telephone with his
father's kidnappers, six
days after the abduction of
Dr. Iglesias in 1981. The
kidnappers, members
of a faction of the Basque
terrorist organization
ETA, demanded
$2 million in ransom.*

police believed that the crime had been committed by
ordinary criminals. But within a few days, the authorities decided that they were dealing with a faction of
ETA, the Basque terrorist organization.

The Basques, concentrated in northeastern Spain
and northwestern France, are an ancient people
whose exact origins remain a mystery to scholars.
Neither their language nor their blood types bear any
similarity to those of other Europeans; theories sug-
gesting that they made their way to Spain and France

from India or the Middle East are plausible but have never been proven. Whatever their origins, the Basques have been in Spain since the beginning of recorded history, and they have maintained their own language and customs throughout the centuries. Their independence has often irked the central government, and this was particularly the case after the Spanish Civil War. The Franco regime, determined to impose uniformity throughout Spain, outlawed the Basque language and severely punished any attempts by the Basques to determine their own affairs. In response, some Basques organized terrorist groups, attacking the police with guns and bombs, leading to an all-out war between the authorities and such organizations as ETA. Even after the fall of Franco, the conflict continued, as the terrorists continued to press for complete independence for the Basque region. (The initials ETA stand for "Eta Ta Askatasuna," which means "Basque Land and Liberty" in the Basque language.)

By kidnapping Iglesias's father, the ETA faction hoped to obtain a large payment from the singer, enabling them to continue their campaign of terror against the government. At the time of the kidnapping, Iglesias himself had no idea who was responsible, but he felt that in some sense he shared the guilt for what had happened to his father. "I cannot ignore the fact that my father was kidnapped because I am his son," he told the press. "It is difficult for me not to feel implicated."

Iglesias indicated immediately that he was willing to pay the ransom, provided that he was given some proof that his father was alive and in good health. Meanwhile, he did his best to console his mother, who had joined him in Miami, and relied on his brother, Carlos, to conduct negotiations with the kidnappers from Madrid. When he was satisfied that his father had not been killed or injured, Iglesias arranged to send his

At a Miami news conference in January 1982, Dr. Iglesias rejoices over his liberation by Spanish security forces. The Iglesiases were criticized for not holding the conference in Spain, but Julio contended that his father had been too exhausted to meet the press before flying to Miami.

brother $1 million in cash in a battered suitcase, which was whisked through Spanish customs in Madrid by special arrangement with the authorities. Carlos raised $1 million worth of pesetas in Madrid.

Meanwhile, the Spanish government was working diligently to uncover the location of Dr. Iglesias, and they traced the kidnappers' telephone calls to Trasmoz, a small town in the province of Aragon. Finally, on the night of January 17, 1982, a special antiterrorist force surrounded Trasmoz, sealing off the town and evacuating the residents of houses nearby the kidnappers' lair, a large residence on the main square. In the early hours of the morning, the security forces swept in, overwhelming the sleeping kidnappers and rescuing Dr. Iglesias.

After spending 19 days locked in a windowless room, the 61-year-old Dr. Iglesias emerged in a state of fatigue but was otherwise in good health. After two

days of rest, he and Carlos flew to Miami for a family reunion. Julio, naturally overjoyed, expressed his gratitude to the Spanish authorities and announced that he was going to set up a special fund to benefit the families of all officers of the Civil Guard (Spain's national police force) who were killed in the line of duty. However, the jubilation of the Iglesias family was marred by a surprisingly critical reaction in Spain. *El País* (The Nation), Spain's most influential newspaper, launched a vigorous attack on Iglesias in the wake of the kidnapping.

In a long editorial, *El País* complained, first of all, that the Iglesias family had shown contempt for Spain by having Dr. Iglesias hold a news conference in Miami rather than on his native soil. The editorial went on to state that the $1 million in the battered suitcase should not have been returned to Iglesias after his father was rescued. According to the newspaper, the singer owed back taxes, and the money should have been kept by the Spanish government as part of his payment.

As Spain progressed under a socialist government that was concerned with narrowing the gap between the haves and have-nots, it was inevitable that Iglesias come in for his share of criticism. More disturbing, in the aftermath of his father's kidnapping, was the knowledge that he could never again be so carefree; he took immediate steps to arrange protection for his parents and also for his ex-wife, Isabel Preysler, and his children. He was also distressed to witness the effects of the ordeal on his father: fearful of another kidnapping, Dr. Iglesias gave up his medical practice and spent two years traveling, never staying in any one place for more than a short time.

On the positive side, Iglesias admitted to an *El País* reporter that he had evaluated his life and had been able to appreciate the importance of his family and

The Iglesiases pose for a family portrait, after being reunited in Miami in January 1982. Julio said that the kidnapping made him realize how much he valued his family and how much he relied on the affection of his fans, thousands of whom had expressed their support during the family's ordeal.

also to understand the price people pay for success. "I think I've paid one of the highest prices of anyone, with interest," he said. Moreover, he had been deeply moved by the many letters he had received from perfect strangers, all of whom offered their prayers and sympathy in his time of suffering. This outpouring of support had helped him to realize how much he valued "the affection of all of you, and I include in that more than anything the appreciation and the applause of the public." With renewed determination, he resumed his efforts to win over the American public, and his efforts soon paid off.

1100
BEL AIR PLACE

Julio Iglesias records in a Miami studio in 1982. With the release of his first U.S. album, Julio, *the following year, Iglesias took a major step toward achieving stardom in the United States.*

Julio Iglesias's breakthrough to the English-language market actually began in England, where he had recorded his first album but had sold very few records due to the language barrier. That situation changed in 1982, when he released a Spanish version of Cole Porter's classic "Begin the Beguine." The song had always been popular with the British public, and when British tourists traveling in Europe heard Iglesias's version, they responded; his decision to begin the song in English before switching to Spanish added to its appeal for English speakers. Before long, the disc was being marketed in England, selling more than 500,000 copies. CBS followed up on the record sales by booking Iglesias into London's Royal Albert Hall for five separate concerts. The Spanish star appeared to have no problem at all communicating with the British audience, which responded rapturously to his voice, his looks, and his showmanship.

Clearly, the time was right for an all-out assault on the U.S. market. The first step Iglesias took was to hire a public relations firm to get his name into the media in a positive light. He chose Rogers & Cowan, a Los Angeles firm that also represented such pop music stars as Paul McCartney, David Bowie, Olivia

Newton-John, and Cher. The firm's job was to make sure that the American public got to know Iglesias as a person and a public figure, thus arousing their interest in him as a performer.

Rogers & Cowan's first major move on Iglesias's behalf was to book him as the headline performer at a major Los Angeles charity benefit hosted by the actor Kirk Douglas and his wife, Anne. The event turned out to be a glamorous affair, with more than 200 Hollywood stars attending. Iglesias dazzled the guests with both his performance and his generosity: he accepted no fee, provided a full orchestra at his own expense, and contributed $60,000 to the charity. "About 100 stories came out about it," recalled Warren Cowan, Iglesias's publicist. "And it made him an instant name here in Los Angeles and around the country. . . . Almost an instant overnight awareness of Julio Iglesias."

Following up on this publicity coup, Rogers & Cowan got Iglesias a guest appearance with Johnny Carson on "The Tonight Show." No doubt eager to do a good turn for the influential public relations firm, Carson went out of his way to make Iglesias feel comfortable, which was especially important because the singer was still not completely at ease speaking informally in English. As a fellow performer, Carson also felt a genuine admiration for Iglesias and his achievements. "He has a stage presence that is just remarkable," Carson marveled, "and I have rarely seen anyone whose command of an audience is so total."

Iglesias diligently made the rounds of celebrity parties, having his photo taken with fashionable and powerful people and getting his name into the society pages and gossip columns. But all this media exposure would not have meant a great deal if he had not also shown the American public why he had sold tens of millions of records throughout the rest of the world.

Iglesias chats with film legend Kirk Douglas at a Hollywood gala. Along with his Belgian-born wife, Anne, a longtime Iglesias fan, Douglas introduced the singer to many important society and show business figures in the United States.

Realizing this, CBS released *Julio,* an album of previous Iglesias hits, some in Spanish and some in English. The appearance of the album was coupled with a four-night engagement at New York's cavernous Radio City Music Hall. The concerts were completely sold out, and the event had the look of a major society affair, with spotlights sweeping the night sky above Manhattan and the sleek limousines of the city's elite double- and triple-parked outside Radio City. In the wake of Iglesias's triumph, sales of *Julio* topped 1 million; fans were clamoring for the record not only in New York and Los Angeles, where there were many Spanish speakers, but also throughout the Midwest and the South.

Iglesias's efforts in the United States did not cause
him to forget that the rest of the world was eager to
hear him, too. During 1983, he also performed in
Mexico and embarked on a record-breaking tour of
Japan. Finally, he spent the latter part of the summer
touring Spain, where he performed for King Juan
Carlos and Queen Sofia; in addition to this honor, he
finally fulfilled his dream of performing in Real Ma-

drid's home soccer stadium—instead of defending the goal, however, he was singing to 70,000 fans who were not the least bit affected by the criticism Iglesias had endured in the nation's press.

On September 23, Iglesias reached his 40th birthday. Rogers & Cowan saw the opportunity to turn the milestone into a celebration of Iglesias's stature in the entertainment world, and the firm staged a lavish

Iglesias celebrates his 40th birthday at the Pré Catalan restaurant in Paris, where the festivities included a spectacular birthday cake. Later in the evening, Iglesias received the Diamond Disc Award, commemorating his achievement of selling 100 million record albums.

affair in Paris. The people of the city were eager to honor the Spanish singer. Paris's mayor, Jacques Chirac, declared September 23 Julio Iglesias Day and presented Iglesias with the Medal of Paris in a special ceremony. In the evening, 500 select guests attended a dinner in Iglesias's honor at the Pré Catalan restaurant in the Bois de Boulogne. The highlight of the dinner was a unique award bestowed on Iglesias by the publishers of the *Guinness Book of World Records.* Rogers & Cowan had informed the publishers that Iglesias had become the first performer in history to sell more than 100 million record albums. The Guinness people had not only recorded this feat in their popular reference book; they had created the Diamond Disc Award, a gold record studded with diamonds, and capped the evening's festivities by presenting the glittering trophy to Iglesias.

Selling 100 million albums was a remarkable achievement, but it did not in any way take the edge off Iglesias's ambitions. He had not yet realized one of his major projects: to release an English-language album that was produced and recorded in the United States. Part of his preparation was a concerted effort to master English, which he practiced diligently with a private instructor. At the same time, he was becoming acquainted with leading U.S. record producers, music arrangers, and performers, searching for the best supporting talent for his American record debut.

One of Iglesias's least predictable and most valuable contacts turned out to be the country music star Willie Nelson. Nelson had heard Iglesias's recording of "Begin the Beguine" during a visit to London. When he returned to the United States, he phoned Iglesias to express his admiration. The first meeting between the two singers got off to a comical start; when the elegantly dressed Iglesias went to Nelson's house, he was greeted by a bearded man wearing a

Iglesias and Willie Nelson perform Albert Hammond's "To All the Girls I've Loved Before" at the 1983 Country Music Awards ceremonies, in Nashville, Tennessee. Their recording of the song was both a hit single and a highlight of Iglesias's breakthrough U.S. album, 110 Bel Air Place.

T-shirt, jeans, and a bandanna, and he assumed that this was the Nelsons' caretaker. In fact, it was Nelson himself, dressed in his customary outfit. Iglesias and Nelson quickly adapted to one another's styles and agreed to cut a record together. The resulting single, "To All the Girls I've Loved Before," featured a fascinating blend of Iglesias's velvety voice and European accent with Nelson's rough but pleasing Texas twang. The unusual combination captivated both country fans and those who usually preferred traditional ballads, gaining new admirers for both artists.

"To All the Girls I've Loved Before" was one of the key ingredients in the new U.S. album, *1100 Bel Air Place,* which Iglesias released in 1984. The album, which bore the address of the house Iglesias had lived in while making the record in Los Angeles, also featured an opening duet with Diana Ross, "All of You." The rest of the the album was a skillful blend of U.S. and European material, sung completely in English. Combining the efforts of so many talented individuals on the U.S. recording scene, adding the sure touch of Ramón Arcusa (who knew Iglesias better than anyone), and polished by Iglesias's fanatical perfectionism,

In a typical gesture, Iglesias acknowledges the applause of a concert audience in 1983. Reacting to suggestions that he exploit his romantic appeal by acting in films, Iglesias responded firmly, "Julio Iglesias does not belong in the movies. Julio Iglesias belongs on a stage, singing."

1100 Bel Air Place was an immediate hit, selling more than 1 million copies during its first five days in the record stores. In addition to upping Iglesias's total in the *Guinness Book of World Records,* the album completed a remarkable transformation. Just two years earlier a virtual unknown in the United States outside Spanish-speaking communities, Iglesias was now one of the hottest properties on the entertainment scene.

"WARRIORS DIE IN BATTLE"

The proof of Iglesias's new status came quickly on the heels of his 1984 breakthrough into the U.S. market. Few people are more aware of public sentiment than the marketing experts of international corporations, and as Iglesias's career continued to grow, he got the attention of the leading executives at Coca-Cola. Engaged in a perennial battle with Pepsi for the number one spot in the worldwide soft-drink market, Coca-Cola was searching for an answer to Pepsi's new media campaign featuring Michael Jackson. Believing that Iglesias had an equally large international following, Coca-Cola signed him to a lucrative three-year deal: under the terms of the agreement, Iglesias was to endorse Coca-Cola's products in commercials, and the company was to sponsor his various world tours. The contract was reputed to be worth anywhere from $5 million to $20 million.

Iglesias began by touring North America, stopping in cities as far apart as Boston, Los Angeles, Milwaukee, Denver, Houston, New Orleans, and Toronto, and ending with a weeklong engagement at Radio City Music Hall. At every stop, he sang to large and enthusiastic crowds, even in those locations where very few Spanish speakers lived. "A year ago, someone asked me when I would consider myself a success in America," Iglesias told an interviewer. "I told him I'd be happy

Iglesias enjoys a moment of relaxation at his Miami home in 1988. Still a sports enthusiast, the singer was closely involved in the successful campaign to establish the Miami Heat basketball franchise in South Florida.

on the day I put 10,000 people together in Ohio. In Cleveland [during the 1984 tour], I got 20,000." There were no longer any questions about his ability to conquer America.

Iglesias was by now almost as much a part of the American scene as Coca-Cola itself. He performed several times at the White House at the request of President and Mrs. Reagan—who regarded him as a personal friend—and no one thought it the least bit odd when he turned up at the Washington Monument for an all-star July 4 celebration. Typically, Iglesias did not feel that he had accomplished all that he set out to do. "I have 60 albums in the world, and only one English album," he told an interviewer in 1985, by which time *1100 Bel Air Place* had sold more than 3 million copies. "It's not enough."

Before tackling his next English-language recording project, Iglesias took a break from his punishing touring schedule and spent most of the year at his home in the Bahamas. Even though he was not zipping all over the world in his private jet, he was still filling his time with work. His major project for the year was a new album, entitled *Libra*. The album was intended for Iglesias's core audience: all the songs were in Spanish, with the exception of Cole Porter's "I've Got You Under My Skin." When Iglesias felt the urge to wander during 1985, he usually did so in order to raise money for charitable causes. One of his major efforts was a telethon for the benefit of the residents of Armero, Colombia, whose homes had been destroyed by the eruption of a volcano. He also traveled to France, where he organized a publicity campaign warning young people about the dangers of drugs.

In the following year, Iglesias continued his charitable work by taking the post of honorary chairman of the American Muscular Dystrophy Association, and he also appeared with Willie Nelson and other pop

A helicopter lifts a survivor from the ruins of Armero, Colombia, in November 1985. After Armero was wiped out by a mudslide that followed a volcanic eruption, Iglesias organized a telethon to raise money for the victims.

music stars in the Live Aid concert, which benefited Africans suffering the effects of famine. He also traveled to Mexico City for a special concert marking the 80th birthday of the popular Mexican singer Pedro Vargas, who had given Iglesias a helping hand when the young Spaniard was still relatively unknown.

However, Iglesias had no intention of becoming a performer who did the occasional benefit or television special and spent the rest of his time making records and relaxing. The essence of his art was communicating with live audiences, and he returned to it with a vengeance. After a tour of Japan, he covered the United States from coast to coast, giving 93 concerts in 47 different cities, in a span of 140 days. During this time, Iglesias continued to work on his second English-language album, which was finally released in

1988 under the title *Nonstop.* The centerpiece of the album was "My Love," a duet with Stevie Wonder that became a hit single in both the United States and Great Britain.

Iglesias had been even more obsessive than usual during the recording process, doing so many retakes that the production costs soared to a near-record $3 million. In this case, his drive for perfection may have robbed the album of some spontaneity. Whatever the reason, record buyers did not respond to *Nonstop* as they had responded to *1100 Bel Air Place.* Iglesias took the relatively disappointing sales figures very personally. In a later interview, he admitted that he had gone through a period of depression, during which he questioned the value of his work and everything else in his life. However, he firmly denied rumors of a suicide attempt, indicating that he had regained his balance with the help of a psychiatrist and a healthy routine of physical exercise, including a great deal of swimming.

Despite his disappointments, Iglesias had many reasons to celebrate in 1988. On July 18, he gave a concert in the bullring at Benidorm in order to commemorate the 20th anniversary of his first major step as a performer, his victory in the 1968 Benidorm Festival. He achieved another first on the other side of the world, in Beijing, China, when he became the first foreign artist to be featured in a special program on Chinese television. The estimated total of viewers—more than 400 million—had to gratify even the always-dissatisfied Iglesias.

In 1989, Iglesias was named special representative for the performing arts by the United Nations Children's Fund (UNICEF), which seeks to help disadvantaged and endangered children throughout the world. To give focus to these efforts, the members of the United Nations declared 1989 the Year of the

Julio Iglesias and Frank Sinatra socialize at a 1986 benefit for the Palm Springs Desert Hospital in California. Though sometimes called "the Spanish Sinatra," Iglesias has in fact surpassed Sinatra and all other current performers in worldwide record sales.

Child. Throughout the year and thereafter, Iglesias traveled the world at his own expense, visiting such nations as Korea, the Philippines, Turkey, and the former Soviet Union. In each location, he organized benefit concerts and spent time with underprivileged children. "The world has given me so much," he remarked. "I am able to live my life in song, and my work with UNICEF is, in a small way, my way of repaying my debt. It's one of the great honors of my life."

The strains that had sometimes afflicted Iglesias during the mid-1980s appeared to have lifted when

Iglesias greets a young fan during Miami's Hispanic Heritage Week celebration in October 1983. Beginning in 1989, Iglesias devoted much of his time to working on behalf of children throughout the world under the auspices of the United Nations.

he released his third English-language album, *Starry Night,* in 1990. He was far more relaxed during the recording process, finishing the project at a fairly reasonable cost—for the record industry, at least—of $500,000. As a sign that Iglesias had gained confidence in the loyalty of his U.S. audience, he did not include a duet with a recognized American pop star on the album. The songs he chose to record were among his personal favorites, and all were associated with singers he had admired through the years. He began the album with an Elvis Presley hit, "Can't Help Falling in Love," and moved on to such classics as the Beatles' "And I Love Her," Ray Charles's "Crying Time," and Nat "King" Cole's signature tune, "Mona Lisa." "Everyone from China to Finland knows ['Mona Lisa']," Iglesias remarked, "and nobody can sing it like Nat 'King' Cole. But I think we made it sound very contemporary." The last quality was especially appreciated by critics. Writing in the *New York Times,* Stephen Holden cited Iglesias's "breakthrough performance" on "When I Need You," a song written in part by Albert Hammond, the author of "To All the Girls I Loved Before": "At several moments, the singer drops his formal Mediterranean manner and belts in a voice that has a rockish spontaneity."

Despite the criticism he had endured in Spain, Iglesias had never lost his love for his native country nor his desire to perform for the Spanish people. In 1992, Spain was the focus of international attention due to the Olympic Games in Barcelona and Expo '92 in Seville, commemorating the 500th anniversary of Christopher Columbus's first voyage to the New World. To no one's surprise, Iglesias added his own luster to the summer's festivities with a tour of 23 Spanish cities, highlighted by a performance in Seville's main bullring. The tour coincided with the singer's new Spanish-language album, *Calor* (Heat),

which featured a number of songs made popular by the legendary Argentine tango singer Carlos Gardel. Returning to his recording studio in the Bahamas, Iglesias recorded the new album in French, Portuguese, Italian, and German versions.

By 1993, Iglesias had sold an astounding total of more than 160 million records throughout the world. There appeared to be little more for him to accomplish, but he still continued to put in 18-hour days. Even when not on tour, he began his day by reading several newspapers, taking calls, and answering letters;

Though he has achieved everything he could have hoped for, Iglesias has no intention of scaling down his hectic schedule. "I will be a singer until I die," he told an interviewer. "At the end of my life, if there's nothing else, I will sing in a little theater in Paris with 100 people in the audience."

after a late lunch, he would work out in the gym for two hours or more and then devote himself to recording in the studio or developing new material. When a group of Spanish journalists from Galicia visited him during the summer, they found him typically energetic and—much to their delight—thoroughly Galician in his lack of self-importance, his sense of humor, and his attitude toward work. He also had his ancestral region very much in mind, indicating that he was working on some Galician songs and planned to give a free concert in Galicia later in the summer. The journalists asked him about reports that he was planning to buy a *pazo,* a Galician country estate, and he noted wryly that he had looked into it but found that potential sellers always raised their prices when they knew he was interested. "Do you know any single women who own pazos?" he asked.

Following up, the journalists wondered whether he was finally planning to retire and take life easy. Iglesias's response was immediate: "You can never talk to a warrior about retiring. Warriors die in battle, whenever possible, and in my case, I hope it will be onstage."

SELECTED DISCOGRAPHY

1968   *Yo canto*

1969   *Todos los días un día*

1970   *Soy*

1970   *Gwendolyne*

1971   *Como el alamo al camino*

1972   *Río rebelde*

1973   *Así nacemos*

1974   *A flor de piel*

1975   *El amor*

1975   *A México*

1976   *America*

1976   *En el Olympia*

1977   *A mis 33 años*

1978   *Mi vida en canciones*

1979   *Emociones*

1980   *Hey*

1981   *Momentos*

1982   *De niña a mujer*

1982   *En concierto*

1983   *Julio*

1984   *1100 Bel Air Place*

1985   *Libra*

1988   *Nonstop*

1990   *Starry Night*

1992   *Calor*

CHRONOLOGY

1943 Born Julio José Iglesias de la Cueva on September 23, in Madrid, Spain

1947 Enrolls at College of the Sacred Heart in Madrid

1962 Becomes starting goalkeeper for junior team of Real Madrid soccer club

1963 Suffers serious spinal injury in auto accident

1964 Undergoes operation to repair his spine; spends next three years recovering from paralysis; begins to play the guitar and write songs

1967 Studies law at Cambridge University in England; performs his songs in college pubs

1968 Wins first prize at Benidorm Song Festival with "La vida sigue igual"; signs recording contract with Discos Columbia; "La vida sigue igual" reaches the top of the charts in Spain; Iglesias records first album, *Yo Canto*

1969 Releases second album, *Todos los días un día;* performs at Viña del Mar Festival in Chile, San Remo Festival in Italy, and benefit for earthquake victims in Guatemala; appears in *La vida sigue igual,* a motion picture based on his life

1970 Wins first prize at music festival in Barcelona; represents Spain with "Gwendolyne" in Eurovision Song Contest; "Gwendolyne" becomes the best-selling single of 1970 in Europe and Latin America; Iglesias tours Spain and Japan

1971	Marries Isabel Preysler; makes first visit to Mexico, Central America, and Puerto Rico; daughter, Chaveli, is born; sales of Iglesias albums reach 1 million
1972	"Un canto a Galicia" becomes the number one record in Europe, Latin America, the Middle East, and North Africa; Iglesias releases his first album in German; Columbia Records names Iglesias its top worldwide artist
1973	Iglesias tours Europe, Latin America, and the United States; album sales reach 10 million; son Julio José is born
1974	Iglesias enjoys triumph at Carnegie Hall concert; releases album *A flor de piel* (Skin Deep)
1975	Son Enrique is born; Iglesias releases albums *El amor* (Love) and *A México*
1976	Breaks box-office records for his performances at Madison Square Garden
1977	Appears before 100,000 people in Santiago, Chile; *El amor* becomes the top-selling album in 44 countries; record sales top 35 million
1978	Iglesias signs with CBS International; records first albums in French and Italian; named artist of the year in 16 nations
1979	Iglesias and Isabel Preysler obtain annulment of their marriage; Iglesias records first album in Portuguese; *Emociones* (Emotions) breaks all previous records for worldwide album sales; Iglesias relocates to Miami, Florida
1981	Dr. Julio Iglesias Puga is kidnapped by Basque terrorists and held for 19 days before being liberated by Spanish security forces

1982   Iglesias's recording of "Begin the Beguine" is a hit in England; Iglesias begins all-out assault on U.S. market; CBS International presents Iglesias with Golden Globe award as top-selling artist; album *Momentos* reaches number one in 90 countries; Spanish magazine *Cambio 16* names Iglesias the personality of the decade

1983   Album *Julio* is released in the United States; Iglesias receives Medal of Paris on his 40th birthday and becomes first recipient of the Diamond Disc Award, honoring him for passing the 100 million mark in album sales

1984   Releases first English-language album, *1100 Bel Air Place;* signs three-year promotional agreement with Coca-Cola

1986   Undertakes 93-concert U.S. tour; performs at Farm Aid benefit and 100th anniversary celebration of the Statue of Liberty; named honorary president of the American Muscular Dystrophy Association

1988   Releases second English-language album, *Nonstop;* becomes first foreign artist to have a TV special in China

1989   Appointed special representative for the performing arts by UNICEF

1990   Releases third English-language album, *Starry Night;* undertakes major tour of Asia

1991   Draws 170,000 people at outdoor concert in Santiago, Chile

1992   Releases *Calor* (Heat), his 67th album; participates in Expo '92 and Olympic Games festivities in Spain

1993   Iglesias's record sales exceed 160 million

FURTHER READING

Adams, Cindy. "Julio Iglesias," *Ladies' Home Journal,* August 1985.

Clarke, Gerald. "Hail the Conquering Crooner." *Time,* September 10, 1984.

Daly, Marsha. *Julio Iglesias.* New York: St. Martin's Press, 1986.

Dougherty, Steven. "Julio Iglesias' Good Life Demands Wine, Women, Song—and More Women." *People,* August 29, 1988.

García, Elizabeth. *Julio.* New York: Ballantine Books, 1985.

Garza, Hedda. *Francisco Franco.* New York: Chelsea House, 1987.

Gundersen, Edna. "The Sultan of Swoon." *TV Guide,* November 24–30, 1990.

Marlowe, John. "A Conversation with Julio." *Miami News,* September 1982.

Miller, Holly G. "Julio Iglesias: Wooing America." *Saturday Evening Post,* December 1985.

Rovin, Jeff. *Julio!* Toronto: Bantam Books, 1987.

Seligson, Tom. "The Crippled Youth Who Became Julio Iglesias." *Parade,* April 26, 1987.

INDEX

ELIZABETH MARTINO is a New York–based freelance writer and editor. She has traveled widely in Europe and has written extensively on Spanish culture, history, and literature.

RODOLFO CARDONA is professor of Spanish and comparative literature at Boston University. A renowned scholar, he has written many works of criticism, including *Ramón, a Study of Gómez de la Serna and His Works* and *Visión del esperpento: Teoría y práctica del esperpento en Valle-Inclán.* Born in San José, Costa Rica, he earned his B.A. and M.A. from Louisiana State University and received a Ph.D. from the University of Washington. He has taught at Case Western Reserve University, the University of Pittsburgh, the University of Texas at Austin, the University of New Mexico, and Harvard University.

JAMES COCKCROFT is currently a visiting professor of Latin American and Caribbean studies at the State University of New York at Albany. A three-time Fulbright scholar, he earned a Ph.D. from Stanford University and has taught at the University of Massachusetts, the University of Vermont, and the University of Connecticut. He is the author or coauthor of numerous books on Latin American subjects, including *Neighbors in Turmoil: Latin America, The Hispanic Experience in the United States: Contemporary Issues and Perspectives,* and *Outlaws in the Promised Land: Mexican Immigrant Workers and America's Future.*

PICTURE CREDITS